THE

OF F

PSYCHOLOGY PRACTICE

RICHARD KASPERCZYK

& RONALD D. FRANCIS

First published 1997 by
MACMILLAN EDUCATION AUSTRALIA PTY LTD
107 Moray Street, South Melbourne 3205

Associated companies and representatives
throughout the world

National Library of Australia
cataloguing in publication data

Francis, R. D. (Ronald David), 1931–.
The professional psychology handbook.

{Rev. and updated ed.}
Bibliography.
Includes index.
ISBN 0 7329 4132 6 (set).
ISBN 0 7329 4130 X.
ISBN 0 7329 4131 8 (Manual of private psychology practice).

1. Psychology – Practice – Australia. 2. Psychologists – Australia. I. Francis, R. D. (Ronald David), 1931– . Handbook of professional psychology. II. Cameron, Colin. III. Kasperczyk, Richard. Manual of private psychology practice. IV. Title. V. Title: Handbook of professional psychology. VI. Title: Manual of private psychology practice.

150.2394

Typeset in Century Schoolbook and Helvetica
by Superskill Graphics, Singapore

Printed in Hong Kong

Cover design by The Incredible Sons of Hawaii Five-O

Contents

Acknowledgements

In everyone's career there are special people without whom progress would not have been easy or even possible. One of those without whose persistent support this book would not have been possible is John McCaffery.

The support and encouragement of many other psychologists who have been active in the Private Practice Issues Group in Victoria (which has transformed into the Victorian Section of the APS Division of Independently Practising Psychologists) as well as many other places, is also gratefully acknowledged. Rachel Abramson, Evelyn Field, Pam Martin, Jocelyn Eaves and Greg Nathan belong to the special group of encouragers to whom we offer our thanks. Many callers who posed interesting questions and sought advice in their practices also have made an unsuspecting contribution to this book.

We are grateful to the Australian Psychological Society for permission to reproduce the Schedule of Fees. Special thanks go to Sharon Clifford who has faithfully assisted in researching this and many other projects we have undertaken. The constant support and encouragement of our colleagues is sincerely acknowledged.

RTK and RDF

1 Introduction

1.1 The story behind this book

Psychology has been identified as the fastest growing profession, with the prediction of just over 100% growth in the next 10 years (DEET, 1995). More graduates are expected to enter the market with the view to hanging up their shingle and earning their living by independent means.

At the same time, no corresponding change has been observed in the training of psychologists to manage a professional practice. Support for the psychologist in private practice has not kept up with the demand and expectations. This Manual aims, at least partly, to fill that void. Its ambition is to add to the profession of psychology by providing the practitioner with foundation skills in managing a practice. On the more practical and less altruistic side, the authors, along with quite a few other practitioners, expect to spend less time in answering the questions from those starting out, as many of the answers are contained in this Manual.

1.2 The target reader

The Manual has been written with a wide reader audience in mind, ranging from students who contemplate working in private practice through to the very experienced practitioners who would like to either expand or sell their practices. The readers who are likely to benefit most, however, will be the psychologists who are serious about planning the establishment of their private practice.

1.3 Relationship with *The Professional Psychology Handbook*

This Manual has been designed as a companion to *The Professional Psychology Handbook* (Francis & Cameron, 1997), and so it is useful to compare and contrast the two. While there is obviously some overlap in the issues covered, this book deals almost exclusively with the business side of setting up, managing, expanding and selling the practice. The Handbook, on the other hand, is more general, and addresses professional issues that are equally relevant to psychologists beginning their careers, as well as those in all types of employment, including private practice. This Manual, therefore, will assume the professional knowledge of psychology included in the Handbook.

1.4 Defining 'private practice'

The terms 'private practice' and 'independent practice' will be used interchangeably throughout this book. They both mean the type of employment that involves generating income through independent means, that is, not through being employed by any organisation. Private practice embraces those who practise on a part-time basis even if they obtain income from other jobs such as lecturing, and counselling in community centres or hospitals on a salary or contract basis.

1.5 The road map of the Manual

This Manual will take you through the whole journey of private practice, from thinking about starting it (Chapter 2), through its development, planning and establishment (Chapters 3 and 4). By the end of Chapter 4, you are presumed to have a basic practice in operation. The next steps involve stretching you towards more business-like approaches: pursuing excellence (Chapter 5) and strategies for expanding the practice (Chapter 6). In the latter chapter you will find more elaborate marketing ideas.

The journey ends with selling the practice (in Chapter 7), which by now should be a thriving business worth much more than it was when you first began. It could be argued, from the business point of view, that what is contained in that chapter should be your aim throughout the development of your practice so that you can reap the rewards of the long-term investment of time, effort, risk and energy that running a practice inevitably entails. You might like to think of your practice as not only a source of satisfaction and income, but also a form of superannuation when you reach retirement age.

A list of resources can be found in the Appendixes as well as some useful samples of the documentation and other resources discussed in the Manual. The Index is designed to help you find quick answers to frequently asked questions.

2
Before starting out in practice

2.1 The fundamentals

The content of this book from here on will assume that you know the basic prerequisites for practising psychology, which are presented in much more detail in the companion of this Manual (*The Professional Psychology Handbook*). In summary these are:

- qualifications gained from an approved psychology course (minimum 4 years plus 2 years of full-time, or part-time equivalent, approved supervision or study in psychology);
- a current registration with the relevant registration board; and,
- if a specialist title is used in practice, the requirement in most states of an additional specialist registration in the relevant psychology discipline (such titles usually include Clinical, Counselling, Educational and Developmental, Organisational, Forensic, Community, Sport, and Clinical Neuropsychology).

While membership of the Australian Psychological Society (APS) may be an advantage, it needs to be understood that it is not a legal prerequisite for psychology practice. Some of the advantages of membership are the recognised credibility and skills gained from the ongoing professional development, the implicit commitment to the APS code of conduct, and association with other professionals.

A further advantage, but also not a legislative requirement, is the membership of the relevant APS colleges (Counselling, Clinical, Organisational, Forensic, Educational or Sports) and the Division of Independently Practising Psychologists (DIPP), which provide valuable opportunities for professional networking and gaining skills in practice management.

Some psychologists also choose to become members of the Australian College of Private Consulting Psychologists (ACPCP), particularly in those states where the college is active in representing psychologists before external fee-setting bodies.

It is also assumed that prior to starting out in private practice the professional is not only qualified, accredited and registered but also skilled and competent to practise. Gale (1990) has articulated the frequent anecdotal evidence that psychology degrees do not necessarily equip the student with the applied skills, particularly for private practice. Conversely, psychology training equips graduates with skills that are marketable in other contexts (e.g. numeracy, literacy, analytical thinking and people management).

It can be argued that professional competence is more critical for private practitioners than for otherwise employed psychologists, simply because it is the clientele, the market, who make a judgement about the practitioner's competence every time they return and every time they pay their fees.

The issues of professional development, peer networks, reviews and support, and accountability for the code of conduct are essential ingredients in the life of a professional in private practice.

2.2 Taking stock

Any career transition or its commencement calls for some vocational introspection, but the move towards establishing your own private practice demands it. Consider the following questions:

- What drives me towards becoming an independent income earner?
- What do I expect to gain from it that I cannot obtain from another job?
- What do I stand to lose from this venture — what are the risks?
- What are my skills — my strengths, weaknesses?
- What opportunities and threats does it pose for me — and which ones outweigh the others?
- How will it affect my life — and am I prepared for this change?

While this book is not meant to discourage you from choosing the private practice option, its message, very simply, is this: do not take this step lightly — it is not as easy as it seems. It is a sobering thought that 80% of all businesses fail within the first year. Psychology business is no exception. If you are to succeed where many failed before, you must be prepared at least for the following:

- some start-up investment, although this does not need to be a lottery win;
- constant uncertainty of income;
- ongoing non-professional tasks, especially marketing and administration;
- professional isolation; and
- perpetual pressure on the availability of time.

Your position, however, does not necessarily need to be a lonely or pressured one, particularly when you are well established and are possibly working in a team of professionals with support staff around you.

2.3 Your motivation

This part of the soul-searching exercise aims to help you decide whether private practice is for you, and if you are not sure, which of the possible alternatives to the solo practice is more suitable.

Check if your desire to enter private practice is motivated by:

- potential for greater income;
- more flexibility in your working conditions;
- the need for independence from others;
- the need to control your life;
- potential investment for retirement; or
- the desire for more challenge in your job.

If your motivation is financial, you will need more patience, as it may take a few years to get there. If, on the other hand, you identify with those who first and foremost desire independence and flexibility, you may relax, as these are relatively easy to achieve. Your destiny, your workload and the level of your income is totally in your hands the moment you step out from the job that pays you regular income.

2.4 Your expectations

Psychologists are trained largely by academics, who have a distinct view of the world. Lecturers operate on the academic model that requires everything to be just so (and that is as it should be in training). In practice, however, it is not a matter of trying to be perfect but rather of trying and mainly succeeding.

As one business owner expressed it — business is a matter of juggling as many balls in the air as can usefully be done, and of dropping the minimum number. When juggling, particularly as a beginner, you will almost certainly drop a few balls. The trick is not to be upset by them, and not to think of them as failures. If you mainly succeed you are still bound to lose some contracts, commissions, ideas and so on. Such losses are learning experiences, and are not to be considered as major setbacks. The overall measure of success is what matters, not that every enterprise you try will get top marks.

Psychologists committed to succeeding in their practice must also be prepared to spend much unpaid time playing multifaceted roles in establishing their practices. An alternative would be to expect to invest a substantial amount of money up front to purchase the services of others specialising in business planning, marketing, administration, accounting, information systems, customer service and so on before the practice is able to afford them. If you are in a position to afford this assistance, the path to financial success is likely to be easier and the end can be achieved more promptly.

In our experience, most psychologists choose to invest their time in lieu of money to reduce their financial risks, particularly when cash is available only through high-interest loans. It must be remembered that expending time on any work-related project or business development is just as valid an investment as the financial one. It can bring much reward and this time should be properly costed into the overall equation of business development. For example, it may be helpful to charge out your time to an imaginary client at a reasonable hourly rate that is equivalent to the lost earning opportunity (say $85), so that the true cost of time-based investment can be tracked. Then the transition into the next stage of business development of releasing the primary income producer into the consulting rooms can take place more easily.

One way or another, unless you expect to invest something of yourself (time, money, commitment and emotion) you are not likely to succeed. It is helpful to adjust your expectations by talking to other practitioners about their early experiences (most of us love talking about ourselves).

Realistic expectations will lead you not to overestimate your potential income in terms of the number of counselling or training sessions you can undertake without suffering burnout. The more realistic you can be at this early stage of planning, the easier you will find it to survive after the glow and excitement of the honeymoon stage of business development have all but disappeared, some months or years later.

2.5 Your skills and interests

In addition to technical skills and professional competence in the relevant area of psychology, there are two other skill clusters that often determine whether a private practice will be successful. These are enterprise and business management. The enterprising cluster has to do with confident presentation of yourself and your product (selling and loving it!), and the business management includes strategy development, planning, administration and financial management.

If these seem daunting and unfamiliar terms, there is no need to be alarmed as such skills can be relatively easily acquired as long as you are determined to acquire them. If you cannot locate such determination it may be because your vocational interests simply do not lie in this area.

This should not be a surprise: after all, you have chosen psychology as your profession.

Succeeding in private practice starts with a clear recognition of one's strengths and weaknesses and the subsequent wise choices. Your lack of interest in business does not automatically disqualify you from running a private practice. You need to know your limits and compensate for them by seeking the assistance of trusted professionals or choosing an alternative to a solo practice that demands the balancing act of all three skill clusters (technical, enterprising and business).

It may also be helpful to remember that the study of psychology involves all aspects of human behaviour, including running a professional business. Some of the cognitive skills that form a part of our repertoire for improving human performance can be very effectively applied to succeeding in private practice.

2.6 The alternative options to solo practice

All too often psychologists choose to start their practices on their own even though their mix of skills is incomplete. The result can be either an unexpected discovery of a hidden talent or, more likely, one of two often observed outcomes. The first is failure to sustain the practice in the long term. The second is an ongoing impoverished practice which, although financially unrewarding, is continued because of personal commitment or lack of other opportunities.

At this early stage of considering entering private practice and conducting a personal skill audit it is wise to consider other alternatives to solo practice.

2.6.1 Ask someone to join you

The most obvious alternative is to work with someone else who can complement your skills in the areas of marketing or business management. While this seems to be an easy option, utmost care must be taken in the choice of a partner, and with the necessary legal contract documentation. The legal partnership is addressed in more detail in Chapter 3.

It is useful to consider such an arrangement in its simplest form; that is, where everything is shared equally, including income, with the practitioners allocating time to the areas to which they are best suited.

Problems are bound to arise unless all expectations of each other's roles and financial arrangements are clearly articulated and formally agreed upon before starting. There can be no easier grounds for disagreement between partners than a perception that one's financial reward is not commensurate with one's effort. For example, while most of the business is generated by one partner, both partners share the income equally; or one partner may have invested more time at the start of the practice because the other was still in full-time employment.

The effort that goes into marketing must be adequately recognised and rewarded. This topic is further explored in Section 3.3 in the context of choosing partnership as a business structure.

2.6.2 Share administration

Another version of a joint practice, particularly useful when business management skills are scarce, is to enter an arrangement with another psychology practitioner whereby the administration is shared but the practices are separate. This model is akin to a medical practice where the reception area and all business systems are shared. The individual practitioners derive their separate incomes commensurate with the number of clients they see and the fees paid by those clients.

The administration costs, which may include marketing of a practice, office-related costs, reception and support staff, and so on, are shared either equally, or in proportion to the business size of each practice, for example the area occupied or administrative effort utilised.

2.6.3 Buy into an existing practice

A more costly but easier option is to buy an existing psychology practice or even buy a share in someone's established practice. In this way, all the administration systems would be expected to be in place and proven to be effective. To minimise the risk of such a decision it is recommended to seek advice of a professionally qualified accountant with experience in auditing professional service businesses. This issue is tackled in more detail in Chapter 7 on selling your practice.

2.6.4 Use other professional's established systems

Rather than buying into a psychologist's practice, a viable alternative may be to enter into a similar administration-sharing arrangement. This is either renting a serviced office or sharing with a professional whose business is other than psychology. That person may already have the rooms and reception systems set up. This arrangement can take the form of a 'serviced office option' or an informal subleasing option. The practicalities of each of these options, such as expected costs, are covered in more detail in Section 4.4.

The choice of a professional with whom administration could be shared would depend on your requirements for the client interface systems. Health professionals (chiropractors, medical specialists, physiotherapists and general practitioners) would be most suitable for counselling or clinical psychology practices. Management consultants, business trainers, accountants or lawyers can also be potential administration-sharing partners, particularly for organisational psychologists.

One added advantage of such an arrangement is a potential for interdisciplinary client referrals and networking. Having other active and like-minded people around you when you work is a far better environment to succeed in than sitting on your own in a home-study. There are other significant indirect benefits from sharing a business administration with another professional. Not the least of these is the ability to immediately present a professional image to the clientele without prohibitive set-up costs. The feel of an established and successful practice should not be underestimated. It can be a very important factor in how positive you feel about the worth of your services, and that beneficial confidence may well flow on to your marketing.

2.6.5 Form a consortium

Another variation of partnerships is a consortium of a number of psychologists who pool their resources to set up their independent practices and collectively market them. Access to a larger pool of resources means that a marketing consultant can be hired and glossy brochures printed.

All the warnings about partnerships that were sounded above must be repeated for this option — this time using a loudspeaker. Given the nature of a consortium arrangement and an unpredictable work flow, some members may do very well while others may not have much work at all. The basis of income sharing must be meticulously addressed prior to starting such a venture to avoid unnecessary pain and losses (in legal fees) after the initial glow and enthusiasm fade.

It is strongly recommended that all arrangements involving partnerships, administration sharing and consortia are constructed with the assistance of legal specialists.

2.7 Your attitude

From here on, this book will assume that you are ready to start a private psychology practice. So, before plunging into the torrent of advice and practical hints, let us delve for a moment into your attitudes towards business, private practice and earning income.

The authors offer no apology for their assumptions, which underpin this whole book, that a private practitioner is committed to quality of service. By 'quality' is meant professionalism of the highest standard, a desire to continuously improve achieved standards, and unequivocal commitment to ethical behaviour. None of these commitments can be subservient to the financial imperatives; that is, they cannot be traded for the desire to make more money. If this were to happen, the short-term gains would soon give way to long-term losses or underachievements.

The profession of psychology is young compared with, say, medicine and law — public acceptance of a psychologist in private practice being even more recent. Therefore, it is our collective responsibility to ensure that the increasing credibility gained by, and trust placed in, psychologists is not undermined by practices that do not measure up to the professional standards expected by our increasingly sophisticated society.

An important component of the attitude to quality and professionalism is the practitioner's belief about the intrinsic worth of his or her services. If you are about to provide psychological 'products' to the marketplace you must be assured that their quality is such that they are worth paying for.

It is often said that a business 'product' is differentiated from a 'service' by its ability to be dropped on one's foot. It may therefore be more logical to refer to what psychologists do as service. However, it helps to sharpen our thinking about our practice as a business to think we are providing tangible products. If we do not believe our product is worth buying or, worse, if the quality of the product is not up to scratch, we cannot seriously expect clients to purchase it.

Another attitude that will become a determinant of your success is related to whether you think of your practice as a business, a lifestyle or a hobby — something you do because you like doing it. The ideal is a healthy balance of these concepts. It is vitally important that the practitioner has some insight into the fact that a business venture is being started.

Such an attitude will direct your behaviour towards those areas that may not come intuitively to a psychologist, such as marketing plans, analysing balance sheets and cash flows. If your attitude is such that you would rather not become involved in such 'mundane' activity, then a more realistic option for you may be to remain in employment or at least join with others — do not do it alone.

3
Planning your practice

3.1 Choosing the market

The market is defined here as the group of people to whom you expect to sell your services. This target population will be determined by your area of expertise, being a mixture of qualifications, experience, competence and credibility.

If you have more than one specialty, and find it difficult to decide which one to offer in private practice, consider the profile, and therefore credibility, which you may enjoy in your potential marketplace. For example, you may be better known for your forensic work among solicitors, even though you are also competent at marriage counselling but with a much lower profile among a smaller clientele. It would be prudent to maximise the immediate potential income by concentrating first on the area in which the referrals are easiest to generate.

Your accounts will soon show you what the marketplace values. No matter what you think you are good at, the marketplace will send an unmistakable message that is plain to read. You may think that you are good at assessments, but the marketplace may tell you that you have a gift for phobia treatment or personnel selection. In our experience the marketplace tells you which of those things are financially rewarding.

In choosing your particular area of practice, you may also consider that the most profitable businesses seem to find their niche in the market and perfect those services to that niche rather than attempt to be 'everything to everyone'. Although it may contradict the conventional wisdom, there are plenty of stories about highly successful businesses that specialise in just one product. The downside of such a specialisation could be the lack of professional development in other areas in which the practitioner also has an interest. The danger of monotony has to be weighed up against the need for speedy success.

In reality, psychologists tend to concentrate on more than one area to maintain their interest, motivation and a reasonably broad referral base. Such a strategy also ensures against the potential collapse of a one-income source. Claims of expertise in too many areas may be interpreted as expertise in none. The old joke about when starting a practice, 'a client is anyone who is warm, vertical and has a chequebook' cannot be used as the basis of a successful enterprise.

3.1.1 The alternatives

The diversity of psychology as a profession is reflected in the many opportunities for private practitioners. The major service options currently offered and able to be foreseen are presented in Table 3.1, along with the description of market populations and respective referral sources.

Table 3.1 *Alternative areas of practice*

Practice type	Market population	Referrer source
Organisational	• Employees • Managers/Supervisors • Job seekers • Entire organisations • Teams/Departments	• Executive directors • Management • Training managers • Human resource managers
Counselling/Clinical	• General public • Families • Compensation claimants • Crime victims • Employees	• Self • Medical practitioners • Community health centres • Rehabilitation providers • Insurance agents • Human resource managers • Management • Employee assistance managers • Courts • Solicitors
Forensic	• Compensation claimants • Offenders • Plaintiffs • Defendants	• Solicitors • Courts • Compensation agents
Educational/ Developmental	• Students • Potential students	• Schools • Parents • Self • Community health centres
Vocational/ Occupational	• Students • Compensation claimants • Outplaced employees	• Schools • Tertiary institutions • Rehabilitation providers
Sport	• Athletes	• Sport clubs • Sport associations • Self • Sport club coaches

3.1.2 Market research

Many psychologists are employed by market and social research organisations for their recognised research ability. Those about to bet their future incomes on the success of their practices sometimes forget that they too possess skills to research their markets before beginning.

It is well known that if you want to succeed in anything in life it helps if you plan it well. Starting one's business is no different. After deciding on your area of practice the next step must be to find out who your clients are, and what they need.

It pays to keep in mind at all times that the reason your business exists is to service your clients. The concept of 'marketing' often gets bad publicity among the social service professionals because of its confusion with selling. The perception is widespread that selling is somehow demeaning to a professional. Marketing is all about finding out what your clients need and planning ways to satisfy those needs.

While it is tempting to assume that you know what the market wants because of your knowledge of the industry or the particular population, it pays to check your assumptions. Conducting market research can be as simple or as expensive as you wish. The chances are that spending more on expert assistance in this area does not mean you get commensurate benefit.

The following simple steps will make your market research as effective as you need it to be for the start of a small private practice. If you are planning a bigger venture you may need to adjust this list or seek specialist market research advice.

- *Research existing data* Locate as much of the currently available data about your clients and potential referrers as possible. This will include their views about psychologists, types of problems experienced by your target population, how they tend to use such services, and other relevant issues. The useful sources of such data are the Australian Bureau of Statistics, university libraries, local libraries, your state small business centres, and the Census on CD-ROM (Supermap).
- *Network with other practitioners* An amazing amount of valuable knowledge can be amassed by asking other relevant practitioners about their experiences with clients and marketing. Most psychologists tend to freely share the information, as would anyone else when asked about their success. Make sure that you listen attentively and ask the leading questions: 'How do you advertise? How do you find *Yellow Pages* works? How do your clients find out about you?' Alternatively, if you come across a more talkative colleague, just asking a very open question such as: 'What has made your practice successful?' may suffice for the evening. You must first maximise the opportunities of meeting your counterparts — attend as many seminars, conferences, breakfasts, lunches and professional development workshops as you can, specifically for the purpose of meeting other practitioners, particularly at the early stage of your career.

- *Ask your customers* All too often practitioners tend to forget that the best way of finding out about what the customers need is to ask them. A simple question at the beginning of the first session: 'Who suggested that you see me?' may suffice.
- *Use your own network of relevant friends or acquaintances* For example, you may ask a general practitioner: 'What would you find most useful from a psychologist?' or 'To what psychological services would you mostly refer your patients?'. Human resource managers may be a useful source of information for the employee population. Find out what they use psychologists for — for example, selection assessments, psychological assessments or employee counselling. The next question you need to then answer is: 'How can I make it easier for you to refer someone to me?'.
- *Consider sample surveys of your target population* You could do this if your questions are still unanswered through informal means. Remember that the aim of market research is to define as precisely as possible the perceptions of the group of people with whom you would like to communicate about your practice. In the business of selling psychological products, there are usually two such groups — your direct clients, and the referrers of individual clients. Two target groups are human resource/personnel managers (or line managers) actually benefiting from the service, and the executive decision makers approving the expenditure. Since you would like to influence both groups via your brochures, phone calls or letters, it is helpful to know as much as possible about both of them, especially in relation to their perceived needs for psychological intervention.
- *Conduct small trials for specific products* The trials would be conducted as an alternative to formal market research surveys. If you would like to find out whether a particular product, for example a seminar or a group therapy, is acceptable to the market, it may be more cost-effective to advertise it and test the response rather than ask questions about it in a survey. The advantage of this approach is that if your intuition is right you will have an immediate number of clients who sign up as a measure of its success — and therefore your 'market research' (advertising) costs will have been recovered, and possibly some profit made. The obvious disadvantage is that you need to rely on your guesses of what is an acceptable product. You must also be aware of the risk of failing to attract a reasonable number of responses, in which case you may have to face the unpleasant consequences of cancelling the event, and possibly even returning cheques.

The fundamental principle of conducting your market research is to find out what your clients need and how it is best to package the product which satisfies their needs, so that they would purchase it. You need to know precisely how clients can be assisted in seeking your service or making referrals to you. Everything else that follows in the development of private practice will depend on this information, from writing marketing brochures through to preparing reports.

The use of market research extends beyond increasing client referrals. It can also help to choose the right location for the practice.

3.2 Choosing the location

The location of your practice will probably be dependent on the psychology area of your practice, the type of clientele you service, the image you desire to portray and affordability. The results of your market research should have provided you with valuable information on where your clients will most likely be located. This will include whether being close to public transport is important, and how many other psychologists already operate in your geographical proximity.

The conventional wisdom about not setting up businesses too close to competitors does not always apply to psychological practices. There are some notable examples in the metropolitan cities where a number of psychological practices coexist very successfully in close proximity. This is also observed in other service professions, for example law and finance.

Whatever your choice you must consider your clients' perception of your practice location, particularly if you expect them or their referrers to visit your premises. The choice of various venues, with a discussion on their advantages and disadvantages, is presented in more detail in Section 4.4.

3.3 Choosing the business structure

3.3.1 Considering your needs

The choice of a business structure from which your practice will operate depends in the main on your personal financial situation, your taxation position and your preferences. A business or legal structure is the entity through which your business trades with the external world (your clients and your suppliers). You will also need to comply with various government regulations, corresponding to the structure you have chosen.

There are three general types of structures from which you will have to choose to run your practice:

- unincorporated structures such as sole trader or partnership;

- incorporated company; or
- a trading trust.

While you obviously must consult a professional business adviser such as a Certified Practising Accountant (CPA) before making the final decision, it pays to be prepared and to have done some homework beforehand. Accounting language can be rather foreign, and with the added complexity of the taxation system, the choices and implications may seem daunting.

Apart from the brief discussion that follows, there are many small business publications and information centres that may provide valuable resources at this early stage of business planning (e.g. KPMG Peat Marwick, undated).

The choice of a legal structure you will make at this stage is likely to have significant implications on your practice in the future. This form may not be easily changed because of capital gains implications — so choose carefully. For example, if you were to decide that your trading trust or a partnership should become a proprietary limited company you may face a large tax bill because the new company will immediately be of significant value even though no cash has been generated.

Some of the questions you may consider in making your choices are related to your long-term vision for the practice and your personal circumstances. For example:

- Are you planning to operate on your own or do you hope to expand by asking other practitioners to join you?
- What is your realistic income target and can you generate it on your own?
- Do you hope to expand by employing other psychologists and/or support staff?
- If your practice generates a substantial profit, who would you like to benefit from it — you, your family and/or charitable organisations?
- Would you like to provide incentives to others, for example your staff by profit sharing?
- Would you like to invite others to purchase part of the business by injecting capital into it?

Depending on your answer to these and similar questions one structure may have obvious advantages. In general, if you plan to work on your own, sole trading may suffice. If you hope to employ others, either a company or a trust may be more appropriate. If profit sharing among the family or staff is a high consideration on your list, a trading trust is a better option. The flexibility to distribute profit in a discretionary way among either family members or non-profit organisations can be attractive.

If the word 'psychology' is in the name, check with business regulatory authorities. Some jurisdictions require psychologists registration board permission before registering such a name (see also Section 4.1).

3.3.2 Sole trading

The simplest and most immediate way of operating a business is as a sole trader, using your own name or initials. If you use your own name, there is no requirement to register it as a business in most states. In this scenario, you first 'notify' the authorities of your new business status through the taxation return.

3.3.3 Trading under a business name

A more popular and just as inexpensive way of commencing a business is to register a business name with the appropriate state or territory government authority (e.g. Corporate Affairs Office). This action allows you to nominate any name, which may include your name or initials, as long as it has not already been registered by someone else, and it is not subject to other restrictions imposed by the Companies Code. The use of names that imply a connection with the government or a local authority, or that may be offensive, is restricted and requires special approvals.

The process of registering a business name is quite simple and not time consuming. It is most easily done by visiting the appropriate government authority, with a list of preferred business names. Business registration application forms are available and can be completed on the spot, and you can search through already registered names on the provided microfiche or computer terminals to ensure that the name you have selected has not been registered already. This self-search will save time at the counter as the staff conduct a search to ensure that the name has not been registered before, and collect the fee, which is about $60–$100.

An official registration certificate will be forwarded to you and there are requirements to display this certificate in a prominent place at the business location. Registration usually needs to be renewed every 3 years, and you will be notified of the need to reapply for registration or you can simply let it lapse if the business ceases to operate.

Operating under a registered business name requires only those annual returns normally prepared for taxation return purposes. The obvious advantage of sole trading or business name registration is the low cost of set-up and ongoing maintenance of such a structure. The losses can be offset against other income, and PAYE (pay-as-you-earn) tax does not have to be paid if the proprietors draw cash from the business, although taxation must be paid at the end of the year if profits are made. It is relatively easy to transfer the business constituted under a business name to another legal structure at a later stage, although there may be capital gains tax implications.

The main disadvantage of sole trading under your own or business name is that it is difficult to maintain the practice in the event of retirement, disablement or death of the main owner of the business. The owner is also personally responsible for all the business liabilities (debt, contracts, leases and so on). It needs to be noted that personal responsibility applies to a large extent in all structures. The thrust of recent company legislation aims at the accountability of directors of companies and trustees of trusts. Thus, while your personal responsibility for business liabilities needs to be taken into account when choosing a business structure, it cannot be the overriding factor, and you must make yourself fully aware of the extent of your responsibilities, especially when you enter into leasing or other borrowing arrangements that include your personal guarantees.

3.3.4 Partnership

A partnership as a business structure is very similar to a sole trader status in terms of its legal requirements. Apart from the requirements to register the business name and timely notification of the taxation office, there are no other expenses and formalities usually associated with this structure.

The critical aspect of operating under partnership is the choice of a partner and the agreement. It is highly recommended to formulate a specific agreement with professional assistance from a solicitor, to be sure that all eventualities and issues have been clearly documented and agreed. In the absence of such an agreement, the rules of your partnership will be subject to your state's Partnership Act. While there are many examples of successful relationships between partners based on mutual trust and co-operation it is wise not to assume that such a relationship will continue.

There are many parallels between a business partnership and marriage. In both cases, the choice of a partner starts the relationship (often on the basis of other than rational arguments), which needs careful development, nurturing, negotiation and compromises if it is to survive. A business partnership is tested most severely in both financial extremes: lean and rich times. When the going is tough, there is pressure to perform better and to generate more income. During this phase, particularly in the early stages of partnership, there is sufficient enthusiasm to insulate the relationship from friction. It has some parallels in the business relationships in franchise operations. This initial stage has been creatively described by Nathan (1993) as 'The Glee Stage', where you are both excited about the new venture and full of hope for the future. When there are plentiful profits and the time comes to distribute them, the little-researched human characteristic colloquially referred to as 'greed' tends to interfere with the previously existing harmony in the relationship. The relationship is then likely to enter 'The Me Stage' where you may start to think: 'I could probably be just as successful without you' (Nathan, 1993).

It is easy to imagine, for example, a scenario where one partner's efforts (e.g. a seminar or a specific marketing campaign) generated a substantial profit that was not commensurate with the personal efforts of all partners. This situation must be foreseen and clear procedures and expectations documented. Hence, the details of all rules governing the behaviour of partners must be precisely articulated to avoid pain and disappointment, not to mention legal costs or broken relationships.

Not surprisingly, consistent ethical behaviour by all parties is one of the most significant determining factors in a successful partnership.

If you are seriously considering a partnership structure as the basis for your business, it is worthwhile to emulate other successful models of such practices, both in psychology and in other professions, such as law or medicine. Take time to find out how others have solved their difficulties and developed their agreements.

The partners as joint business owners are personally responsible for all the liabilities of the business. This is particularly important to consider when taking out a loan on a joint and several basis, in which case if one partner fails to meet the required repayments, creditors are likely to seek the funds from other partners. Another disadvantage of a partnership structure is its lack of flexibility in transferring ownership to others.

3.3.5 Proprietary company

A proprietary company is a legal structure, which requires the involvement of solicitors or accountants. It takes a few weeks to set up and costs about $800. The documents that govern the functioning of companies are called memorandum and articles of association. There are two ways of obtaining a company: forming a new company or purchasing one 'off the shelf'.

Shelf companies are already registered, complete with all constitutional documents. These companies are available from agents or solicitors. The original registered name is changed to the suitable name chosen by yourself and then registered with the Australian Securities Commission, which issues a 'Certificate of Incorporation on Change of Name'. It is best to let your accountant advise and guide you through the necessary steps in either process. You can obtain direct services from a solicitor or agent listed in *Yellow Pages* under 'Shelf Company Services'.

Under recent legislative changes a company must have shareholder(s), a director and a secretary. Since the director will most likely be shareholder(s), the director can also act as company secretary. At least one of the directors must reside in Australia.

It is assumed here that the company is private and not public. (Public companies are listed on the stock exchange, which usually takes place when finance is raised from the public issues of shares. Such a step is significantly more involved and requires professional assistance.) The private company issues shares and its directors allot shares and approve transfers of subscribers' shares, according to their decisions, which are minuted in the meetings.

Further shares can be issued at a determined value to another person when an injection of finance is required. When people invest in a company, there is usually an expectation of a return on their investment. Each year, a company's profit is assessed for the availability of funds to be distributed as dividend to shareholders. It is important to note that dividends are paid out of profit or accumulated profit, but not out of capital. Thus a company that is not profitable is of little value to its shareholders unless they can count on its capital value improving when they are ready to sell their shares.

The company cannot trade until a certificate of incorporation has been issued. As soon as you receive all the documentation, you will have to hold the first meeting of directors, as required by the articles of association. In fact, there are requirements for holding regular meetings of directors for which official minutes must be kept. This and many other requirements, however, do not have to be daunting, if your accountant continues to provide you with ongoing professional services to ensure you comply with all the company regulations.

There are costs associated with compliance with the requirements of the Australian Securities Commission, which have to be taken into account in addition to the initial set-up costs. These include both direct government charges for annual company returns, of the order of $200, and indirect costs associated with the accounting services, which are around $400 per year.

While it is easy to focus on the disadvantages of the high costs of operating a practice under a company structure, there are also significant advantages. First, tax on company profits is currently 36%, which is significantly lower when compared with the current maximum personal marginal rate of 48%. After tax profits can be retained in the business for further expansion. Liabilities of the company are limited to the company. However, this advantage needs to be qualified since the directors may also be personally responsible for debt that the company cannot repay, especially if they have given personal guarantees for business loans or overdrafts. Two further advantages of company structures are that it is relatively easy to increase ownership in a company, and to continue trading when the founders can no longer work.

There are some disadvantages of company structures other than high initial costs. Company losses cannot be distributed to the shareholders to be offset against their other income. There is also the often forgotten problem with companies limited by shares where a number of psychologist-shareholders commenced practising together with little initial capital outlay. If their venture becomes profitable, the company share price will have increased dramatically even though no actual money was paid. If one shareholder would like to sell shares, the purchase of your own business is likely to cost you a substantial sum of money, which may not actually be available from the business. In such a case, another person may need to be found to purchase those shares.

All such possibilities need to be explored with your accountant. Do not be satisfied with simple and immediate advice on what legal structure your practice requires. This needs to be considered in the light of your future personal, professional and financial goals, for which the business structure should become a vehicle.

3.3.6 Trading trust

The least understood business structures are trusts, the most common of which are discretionary family trust and unit trust.

The costs associated with the initial set-up and ongoing administration are very similar to the company structure (see Section 3.3.5) although the trust may be marginally less. Likewise, all the requirements related to the Australian Securities Commission, including name registration and articles of association, are similar to those for limited companies because there are two entities that are inextricably linked: a unit trust and its corporate trustee. Thus, while the unit is the actual trading vehicle for the practice, it is the trustee (with its directors at the helm) who makes decisions on behalf of the trust.

The correct way of referring to this structure is 'ABC Pty Ltd as trustee for the XYZ Trust', where ABC is any suitable and registered name, and XYZ is either a family discretionary trust or unit trust, with its own appropriate and registered name. Sometimes the phrase 'as trustee for' is abbreviated to ATF, which can be confusing to a visitor to this legal-financial world.

The main difference between this structure and a limited company consists of the way in which profits and taxation on those profits are treated. While the company profits are taxed at the current rate of 36% in the hands of the company, the trust's profits must be distributed in total and these are taxed in the hands of individual beneficiaries. In the case of family discretionary trusts, the beneficiaries are any family members or other organisations (e.g. tax-exempt charities). In the case of unit trusts the distribution of profits is made on the basis of predetermined proportions of units allocated to each unit holder. In addition, special distributions can be made to other parties, as decided by the trustees, in accordance with the relevant memorandum of articles of association.

The implications for taxation must therefore be considered most carefully when choosing between various trust and company structures. If the family has members who can receive reasonable income with little impact on their personal tax situation, the benefits can be quite substantial. Minors currently can receive only $416 per year without paying any tax. Any additional income is then taxed at 66%. Profit distributed to a non-income earning spouse can be quite beneficial when compared with other structures.

A significant advantage of the unit trust is its flexibility in involving other parties in the business without risking its capital base. There are a number of different units that can be either offered or sold, such as profit, voting and capital units. For example, a 'partner' psychologist can be offered a number of profit units, but no capital units (which can remain in the hands of the practice founder). To ensure someone's participation in the running of the business, a number of voting units can be offered with or without profit units. This technique can therefore be a useful vehicle for providing profit sharing or similar incentives for valuable employees or subcontractors.

Disadvantages of the trust structures include their inability to distribute losses to be offset against the beneficiaries' other income, and the costs associated with ongoing administration and compliance with government regulations. Both of these disadvantages are common to limited companies. In addition, banks or other creditors usually demand evidence from solicitors that trusts have been properly constituted and that no changes to their articles of association have occurred, which, at worst, causes minor inconvenience and delays the proceedings.

3.3.7 Seeking professional advice

When selecting a business structure from those outlined above, or any alternative, it is strongly recommended that you seek your accountant's advice. There is also much government-sponsored free or quite cheap advice and material from business-support centres and government-publishing bookshops (see Appendix B for further resources).

The appointment with an accountant comes first, but there is no reason to accept the accountant's initial suggestion, especially if all the implications and terminology are not clear. Ask lots of questions and seek other opinions as part of your initial research. Different business structures suit different people, and there are many different psychologists. You need to evaluate all the costs, taxation implications and alternatives, to be able to make an informed decision that will suit your needs. When you evaluate the pros and cons of the options make sure that you consider your long-term plans, not just the immediate set-up costs.

There are many accountants who specialise in helping business enterprises start and grow; so it makes sense to choose a professional accountant who has a proven track record with this type of business, rather than someone who has the lowest charge rates or who is a family friend.

Your accountant will most likely refer you to a solicitor and possibly a financial planner for further specialist advice, as your changing needs require. It should be remembered that nobody will actually know your business as well as you do. No accountant can be expected to cast visions for your business. Only you can do that, and it is quite likely that if you are high on enterprise skills you already have future visions for your practice.

3.4 Developing a business plan

There are many useful skills and knowledge that psychologists bring to business management from their standard academic training, although many are not aware of these because their application is in a different context. Counselling psychologists have technical skills in helping their clients formulate their personal development action plans; vocational psychologists have skills relating to career plans; and organisational psychologists have skills relating to change management strategies. All psychologists are aware of the cognitive processes, the power of language and visualisation that determine one's effectiveness. Preparing a business plan utilises all of those skills and concepts.

Effective business plans have just as much to do with these psychological concepts as with financial and management ones. Successful business people have learned the power of planning, envisioning the future and evaluating strengths. They also undertake business planning on a regular basis, usually once a year.

3.4.1 Why a business plan?

Businesses that begin with a written and realistic plan are less likely to fail within the first years of operation. This should be the first step in the commencement of a professional psychology practice and then at least an annual event.

If you fail to plan you plan to fail. You might have said that yourself in a different context but it is just as applicable to running a practice. While it is easier to begin 'doing' things rather than planning them, the danger of underplanning is that you spend your time ineffectively — when things get busier you will be involved in so many urgent things that you will not have time to do the important ones.

Formulating a business plan is one of those activities of the non-urgent but important quadrant (Covey, 1993), as presented in Figure 3.1. Its value is often appreciated much later when you evaluate how you spend your time. An immediate and tangible reason for finding a business plan useful is that bank managers and accountants will find it much easier to understand your practice and to evaluate your needs when you present them with a plan that speaks their language.

Figure 3.1 *Time management matrix*

	Urgent	Not urgent
Important	*Quadrant I activities* • Crises • Deadline driven reports • Pressing problems	*Quadrant II activities* • Planning • Relationship building • Recreation
Not Important	*Quadrant III activities* • Phone interruptions • Some mail • Some meetings and reports	*Quadrant IV activities* • Trivia • Time wasters • Some phone calls

Source: Adapted from Covey, 1993.

There are also some less tangible effects that a business plan will have on your practice, even though you never show it to anyone, and even if you yourself do not read it every day. Writing down your cognitive constructs, articulating your vision and planning your goals is a powerful way of focusing and directing your behaviour towards the identified goals.

To summarise, some benefits of formulating a business plan are:

- A business plan focuses your vision for the practice.
- It forces you to clearly identify your products.
- It serves to evaluate your thoughts and ideas.
- It helps to shape your practice's long-term future.
- It helps in your communication with the financial advisers.
- It ensures your resources are spent efficiently.
- It instils confidence in your practice — for those outside and inside the practice.
- It minimises costly mistakes.
- It provides a basis for measuring your performance.

3.4.2 What is a business plan?

A business plan is a document that provides a description of your practice, and concludes with very specific strategies and action points, including financial details. The five simple questions (Samson, 1988) that a business plan purports to answer are:

- Where are we now?
- What business are we in?

- Where do we want to be in the future?
- What changes are necessary to close the gap between the now and the future?
- How do we make it happen?

Its contents, described in more detail in the following sections, are:

- executive summary;
- situational analysis;
- strategic audit;
- objectives;
- strategies (marketing, professional service, and financial);
- implementation plan;
- performance evaluation.

While it is recommended that you involve someone to provide a helpful and evaluative sounding board, you cannot expect someone else to formulate your business plan. You are the only one who knows the answers to the questions that the plan forces you to answer. You may, in fact, employ specialist business advisers to write the document, but do not be surprised when, at the end of the exercise, you will wonder why you paid so much money for someone to write down what you said.

A cost-efficient approach to writing a business plan is to write the first draft by yourself and then present it to someone with business and financial skills (e.g. your accountant). Be prepared to answer all their challenges and questions. Presentation of your plan, your thoughts and strategies is greatly enhanced when someone skilled in business planning assesses it with some independence and objectivity.

The notes below provide detailed explanation of each part of the plan and can be read in conjunction with the sample structure presented in Appendix D. This sample is only one example of a plan structure; you may wish to adapt it to suit your needs.

3.4.3 Executive summary

Most bank managers or other creditors are not likely to read the entire document, and so it is good business practice to produce a summary of key statements and indicators in a one-page summary (executive summary).

This summary may include sections such as:

- historical background;
- vision and mission statements;
- target market and product/service description;
- key objectives and respective strategies;
- key financial indicators and future estimates.

3.4.4 Situational analysis

This section is most relevant to businesses already in practice. The contents of this section may include the following:

- *Historical background* This includes the details surrounding the commencement of the practice — who founded it and when.
- *Products/services* This section is probably the most fundamental aspect of any business and is often rather difficult for psychologists whose services are not tangible. It defines the types of services that your practice provides (the mission statement).
- *The target market* This defines your clients and describes them in more detail: what their needs are and to what extent your products will meet their needs.
- *The total market* This consists of some guesses, possibly based on available population and market research statistics. This section provides information on the entire market available to the practice.

  If it is a counselling/clinical practice, how many people do you expect will need your type of services in your defined geographical area per year? If it is an organisational practice, how many organisations are likely to require your type of services? Consider how much each client is likely to pay for such a service — this will provide you with the total value of the market in which you are about to operate. You should perform this calculation for each of the types of products/services you plan to provide.

  The information gleaned from this exercise will provide you with an objective estimate of the total potential amount available in your market. Considering that other practitioners will already operate in your area of practice and geographical proximity, the next question is how your services and market (clientele) relate to the other providers (your competitors).
- *Other providers* While it is counter-intuitive for psychologists to think of their professional colleagues as 'competitors', it is worthwhile to consider them as such for the purposes of planning your services. Consider whether your services are similar to or different from theirs. Are the clients (your target market) overlapping theirs or is the market distinctly different? If you are planning to provide existing services to the same market, you will be essentially aiming at cutting into their 'share of the market'.

  Fortunately, in the current climate of the need for psychology services there are constantly expanding markets and there is potential to provide services that at this stage are not available; consequently, the issue of competition is not a seriously limiting factor for psychology practices. It is probable that in the foreseeable future the number of services will expand to the point where the practitioners will seriously have to consider the market share they are planning to absorb.

It is, nevertheless, a worthwhile exercise to consider the existing psychology services offered in your geographical area to your target client group. A simple search for various advertisers in the newspapers and *Yellow Pages*, informal networking, and formal market research will all serve to uncover the colleagues against whom you will be potentially competing for business.

This analysis is significant for at least two reasons: geographical location and quality comparison. First, it is useful to be aware of other psychologists operating in the geographical proximity, so that when potential clients (or referrers of clients) mention another psychologist's name you will not appear surprised. Second, it will help you understand how another practitioner operates. This will provide a useful benchmark against which you can measure the quality of your services. This may also lead you to develop a product that clearly distinguishes you from others.

- *Structure* This describes how your business is organised. Initially this may be a simple statement or a one-line description of all the functions you will be performing. As your business grows this will probably become more complex. It is worthwhile to identify at least the different functions that your private practice has to perform to operate as a business. These include:

— professional services;
— finance;
— administration;
— personnel; and
— marketing.

Each of these functions has to be managed so that your practice can run efficiently. In a small practice, it is common for some of these functions to be performed by the same person, by external service providers such as a typist/computer operator, or by part-time and casual staff who provide assistance as needed, and charge at an hourly rate.

The structure also has to do with the management of each function, rather than its operation; so the questions you need to answer are: who is operating, and who is responsible for these functions?

- *Resources* This section describes the sources of all the business needs. The primary resource in a psychology-based business is the professional human resource. You will begin to think here about the people who need to provide the services that are the fundamental product your business sells. While in most practices this will be provided by yourself, also consider staff, subcontractors or locums. Collaboration with another practice group can be helpful when the workload exceeds your capacity to perform the services or when you are unavailable, for example when you are on holidays or attending a conference.

Human resources must also be considered for all the other functions described in the structure above — who will, for example, assist in appointments, responding to calls, administration and financial management when you are not available?

Other resources include premises from which the practice operates and suppliers who provide you with essentials for business.

- *Technology* This comprises machinery, computers, telephones, communication equipment, computer software and psychological test materials. At this point you will identify the current technology that your practice utilises in its operation.

3.4.5 Strategic audit

This section is essentially a critical analysis of how your practice is currently performing. Business management experts have borrowed the concept of a SWOT (strengths, weaknesses, opportunities and threats) from group facilitators — most likely psychologists. Value may be achieved by standing back, by using someone else to talk things through, and by writing your thoughts and conclusions. This calls for some insight into your personal qualities as well, given that psychology practice products are usually so intricately linked to the person delivering them.

Analysis

To analyse how your practice is currently performing, consider the following:

- *Strengths* Identify the services at which your practice excels. Here you will ask: what do we do in our practice that is better than, or different from, anyone else?
- *Weaknesses* List the aspects of your practice that others do better. You need to honestly assess the areas that you feel need improving.
- *Opportunities* Present the untapped potential that your practice has not explored. You will become aware of the areas of service that are not provided by anyone within your market, or new markets for your existing services.
- *Threats* Include all the factors that work against the viability of your practice. These may consist of internal limitations or external pressures, and local issues or global government actions. It is far better to consider the threats and face them so that you can consciously turn them into opportunities.

Current performance

You can complete the SWOT analysis for the overall practice, or complete it separately under these areas of your practice performance:

- service;
- marketing;
- resources;
- financial.

You need to be aware of the actual performance in each of these areas before being able to formulate strategies for improvement and growth.

3.4.6 Purpose

The mission statement must be clearly spelled out in the business plan. This can be done either at its beginning or in the strategic audit section.

Business vision

In formulating the vision statement you will find it helpful to imagine where you would like to see your practice at the end of a reasonably long period of time, say 5 or 10 years. The vision statement succinctly articulates your practice's philosophy and purpose.

Business mission statement

Mission statements have been abused by many in the business world and some have written them because everyone else seems to have done so. The power of mission statements has been demonstrated by those who put substantial effort into formulating them. A mission statement should be a simple and individual statement which motivates and focuses you and those working with you on the activities that really matter in your practice.

One way to begin thinking about such a statement is: 'My practice exists to . . . '. The simpler and more precise a statement is, the more beneficial it is. Do not be afraid to alter and edit the mission statement in the next business planning cycle. Some examples are as follows. We are in the business of:

- improving individual performance of athletes competing in Olympic sports;
- assisting individuals in resolving personal problems in the workplace in small to medium manufacturing organisations;
- providing forensic assessments for a group of clinical psychologists; or
- providing psychological advice to personnel selection agencies.

3.4.7 Objectives and strategies

Each business has its unique factor that enables it to exist in a sustained way. This special capacity for ongoing business viability of a practice probably has a lot to do with the psychologist's competence. However, the business success goes beyond the individual's capability — it is also related to the way the practice is marketed and the way in which service is delivered.

This section articulates the strategies that will ensure the ongoing viability of the business.

Basis for growth

It is important to decide what type of private practice you would like to operate — a single provider relying for all its income on the exertion of one person, a two-person or three-person practice, or a consulting group.

Solo practice has many advantages such as independence of other people, no staff problems, clear control and efficient decision making, as well as some disadvantages such as difficulty in organising a replacement for holidays and no income when you are away from your practice.

In general, there are four options for business growth:

- provision of more existing services into the existing markets;
- development of new services for the existing markets;
- location of new markets for the existing services; and
- development of new services for the new markets.

'Markets' mean client groups and/or referrers of such clients or projects for psychology practices.

Your statement of the basis for growth (or sustainability) will therefore articulate your general objective as to how you plan to continue to be viable in your practice. For example, 'we will grow by developing new products (seminars, specialist counselling or consulting services) to a new group of clients (defined by their location, a demographic characteristic or belonging to a type of organisation)'.

The strategies presented below will specifically address *how* you plan to achieve the above general objective.

Marketing strategy

The marketing strategy is one of the most powerful elements of the business plan and will be addressed again in more detail in Sections 4.7 and 6.2.

If you have identified in your growth objective that you will develop a new psychology product or target a new group of clients, this is the place where you will write down how you plan to ensure that these clients use your services.

Some of the aspects that you may like to cover in this strategy are:

- position in the market (describe your practice image, tone and feel of it, and how you plan to achieve it — how you would like others to think of your practice);
- target market for each service (describe each group as precisely as you can, drawing upon knowledge gained from market research);
- range of products/services you plan to provide (present an analysis of the profit margin each product is expected to contribute out of total sales; if it is a clearly identifiable product such as a training seminar, present a break-even analysis);
- fee-setting approach (describe how you plan to arrive at the fees you will charge for each product); and
- marketing activities (explain how you will actually communicate information about your products to existing or new client groups — by direct mail, advertising, promotion, free seminars, and so on).

In your planning of marketing strategies you may come across the concept of elasticity of demand, which derives from economics and refers to an increase of purchasing where the goods or services are cheaper.

Some caution is needed here, because in professional work fee lowering may produce an unintended effect. Some people believe that the more they pay (within reason), the better the product; so the value you put on your services may, in part, determine public perceptions of what you offer. What you can do is provide something extra — such as a novel service, a conventional service in an underserviced location, flexibility of consulting times, or an array of services acting in concert.

Service strategy

While it is expected that professionals in private practice are skilled and competent to provide the services, you will need to convince others (e.g. bank managers) that you have that capacity and that you have planned other contingencies if you are unable to provide those services yourself.

It is useful to consider in this strategy the following:

- the skills of those who will provide the services;
- the location from which the services will be provided;
- the frequency and scheduling of the services;
- quality assurance of the services; and
- the safety of clients.

Resource strategy

The resource strategy will address human resources required for the practice, but in areas other than direct service provision. It will decide who will perform the functions of administration, office/clinic management, reception, accounting, cleaning and such like.

Other resources, including the rooms, furniture, equipment, psychological tests, computers and other technologies, need to be planned to match the projected growth of the practice. For the new practice, the initial set-up of the physical location from which the practice is conducted will be included in this strategy.

Financial strategy

The details of your strategies for business growth (marketing, service and resources) must be underpinned by a solid financial plan. This part of the business plan provides a link between all your other ideas for development of new services, conducting marketing campaigns and the financial resources. It answers questions relating to how much income you will earn through new business initiatives, how much it will cost you to generate this income and the source of funds.

The financial strategy takes into account your practice's past performance and includes the projections. It may include all or some of the following concepts:

- financial history;
- capital investment estimates;
- profit and loss statements;
- cash flow projections; and
- balance sheets.

Financial history covers trends in profit and loss in the past 3 to 5 years.

Capital investment can be estimated by the shortfall between the expenditure and the income at the end of the first financial year. If some shortfall is predicted, it needs to be covered by capital expenditure. You need to identify the source of these funds in your financial strategy. For example, it could be a bank loan, in which case the interest costs should be built into the overall expenditure. If you plan to use your own savings as capital, it may be worthwhile to calculate the expected rate of return on this investment to compare it with an equivalent investment elsewhere.

Section 3.5 on financial planning covers the last three of the above concepts in some detail, as they comprise the fundamental tools of budgeting.

The sample analysis in Tables 3.2 to 3.5 provides good examples of what should be found in this part of a business plan. If you do nothing else, the most important part to include is a thorough cash flow projection. This statement will show the predicted amount of cash you need to have in the bank to carry on the business.

Implementation plan

Once your strategies are finalised, the next stage in the business plan should consist of a step-by-step action plan for each of them.

It may be helpful to remember that an effective action plan needs to:

- be expressed in specific terms;
- contain realistic statements of action;
- contain achievable time frames;
- identify the person responsible for each action point; and
- define the measure of success.

Your plan needs to cover all the strategies outlined above. Thus it may be divided into the following four parts: marketing, service, resource, and financial.

You will probably find it most efficient to delegate as many steps of the plan as possible to others. It pays to seek out people who are capable of ensuring high-quality outcomes with minimum supervision. For example, you may develop an ongoing relationship with a desktop publisher or a graphic designer who will take most of the responsibility for the printing of your marketing materials and stationery. Your time, efficiently spent with them, will be most productive.

Your implementation plan is likely to be most effective when you incorporate it into your everyday diary planning — in this way you continue to monitor its implementation. When its deadlines are missed you can then readjust the plan, but keep in mind that it will have a flow-on effect on your financial planning. If, for example, your marketing material does not go out on time as estimated, the projected income from the targeted stream of clients will also not eventuate. Thus you will need to adjust the income and expenditure projections in the cash flow analysis.

3.4.8 Monitoring and evaluation

You should monitor the business plan on a regular basis. In practice this will occur only when you recognise its potential power to help you in the development of your practice as a business in a systematic and stress-free manner.

There is room in the business plan itself for stating how you will monitor the implementation of your action plans and strategies and how you will evaluate it; that is, how you will measure its success at the end of a specified period of time. The plan needs to be flexible and it may need to be adjusted to respond to new opportunities and threats.

While it is recommended that your implementation action plan, along with the cash-flow analysis, is monitored and adjusted on a monthly basis, it is normally accepted that the entire business plan should be redeveloped once a year.

If your practice consists of other staff it is important to involve them in the process of business planning. Their involvement will ensure their commitment to growing the business along with you. Since they are part of your business, they can provide valuable input to identifying new opportunities for improvement. It is often easy to underestimate the wealth of knowledge your staff, especially in the reception or general office, have about your clients. Involving your staff will also recognise their significance with consequent morale improvement.

3.4.9 Where to get help?

The process of business planning should not overwhelm you. If your practice is small, you may choose to borrow some concepts from the above discussion, and follow your intuition. There is no doubt that a systematic and professional approach to running a practice calls for some high-level planning. As previously mentioned, there are many experienced and skilful professionals who can assist you in this process. The first stop will probably be your accountant who may introduce you to a professional business adviser.

You may approach a business adviser directly, but it is helpful to keep your accountant involved in all major developments in your practice. There are also some state and federal government-funded small business assistance initiatives that provide free or low-cost advice and publications on business planning. Some helpful addresses are listed in Appendix B.

One such combined federal/state initiative to improve the efficiency of Australian businesses and increase their competitiveness and exports is the National Industry Extension Service (NIES). There are a number of worthwhile training programs and publications under the auspices of this program. Although it tends to be geared towards the manufacturing sector there are many parallels to any business.

3.5 Financial planning

The previous discussion of business planning covered the development of financial strategy in general terms. Financial planning in any business is an ongoing process that must be undertaken with commitment if one is serious about succeeding.

3.5.1 Start-up costs

One way of looking at start-up costs is to make an estimate (possibly using this book as a basis) to determine the minimum amount required to start the practice. A reverse way is to estimate how much you can raise and then see if a practice can be started using that amount. Suppose one were to decide that $10 000 is the maximum available; then the question one would ask is: 'What can be achieved for that amount?' If the financial resources are very limited one would need to carefully rank the start-up requirements.

The highest priority initial costs, without which it would be difficult to start, are the non-reducibles such as registration fees, professional indemnity insurance, accounting and legal services, telephone systems, marketing, printing of stationery and psychological tests. The amounts you spend on the last three of these can vary depending on the available funds. To this, add the need for income to support you while the practice gets going.

Premises are a significant cost, but renting rooms with established clinics will obviate the need for such things as furniture, photocopier, fax, cleaning and so forth. While you pay rent it can be on a start-up basis of one session per week.

A number of psychologists have found suitable rooms, owned by a specialist who was agreeable to lease them for the sessions he was not there. This was not advertised, but the specialist was happy to have the income for his down time as a bonus for what was non-earning time. With careful selection of such premises there might be the added bonus of gaining a good reputation with the specialist — and therefore referrals.

In the initial set-up of your practice, you may find it useful to prepare a separate list of items that will need to be purchased. Then you can include the totals in the expenditure categories in your cash flow projection, for instance under 'Office Furniture and Equipment'.

A sample list of items that you may consider when estimating your initial outlay is included in Table 3.2 (adapted from APS, 1988).

Table 3.2 *Initial practice capital items: A sample list*

Business formation

(Business registration or company/trust formation[1])

Furniture[2]

Professional office/room:[3]

- 1 desk
- 1 desk chair
- 1 filing cabinet
- 2 chairs
- 1 cupboard
- 1 bookshelf
- 1 print/painting
- Plants

General office:

- 2 desks
- 2 typist chairs
- 2 filing cabinets

Reception/waiting room:

- 3 armchairs
- 1 coffee table
- 3 prints/paintings
- 1 counter/desk
- Coffee machine
- Book/information library
- Plants

Kitchen:

- Refrigerator
- 1 table
- 4 chairs
- Miscellaneous

(*continued*)

Table 3.2 *(continued)*

Equipment[4]	
• Telephone system	• Photocopier
• Dictaphone	• Facsimile machine
• Computer equipment	• Video recorder
• Computer software	• Tape recorder
• Printer	• Security alarm system
• Biofeedback machine	
Stationery	
• Files/paper/materials	• Small equipment (staplers etc.)
Tests and materials	
• 5 selected psychological tests	• Tapes
• Books/pamphlets	
Services	
• Accounting/business advice	• Interior decorator
• Legal advice	• Computer advice and set-up
Printing	
• Design and layout[5]	• Compliments slips
• Letterheads	• Envelopes
• Business cards	• Marketing brochures[6]
Marketing/Advertising	
• Newspaper advertisements	• *Yellow Pages*
• Direct mail campaign	

Notes:
(1) Costs will depend on the business structure you have selected.
(2) All expenditure relating to Furniture will not be relevant when you choose to rent premises on a sessional basis or any lease offices that are already furnished.
(3) These figures will have to be multiplied by the number of professional rooms/offices required by the practice.
(4) Some office equipment may be included in the rental of premises, e.g. telephone, security systems and photocopier. Some equipment will be optional depending on your practice needs, for example a biofeedback machine. If the offices are fully serviced your needs for word processing may also be provided.
(5) The cost of design is likely to vary greatly depending on the quality of your stationery, the creative skills of your designer and your ability to make quick decisions about the designs you like.
(6) The cost of marketing brochures will also depend to a large degree on its quality, complexity, the number of colours and size.

An alternative to purchasing the equipment and furniture for cash is leasing from a finance company. Your accountant should be able to advise you on the best lease arrangements or introduce you to a lease broker who can usually get the best interest rates. If you prefer to do it yourself, you can approach banks or other financial institutions and ask for their commercial leasing arrangements.

One advantage of leasing equipment is that you do not have to outlay a large sum of money up front; instead, you make regular payments that can be met out of generated income each month. The other important advantage of leasing is that it is tax deductible. On the other hand, the disadvantage is the higher cost of interest, which makes the equipment you purchase more expensive, especially since you usually cannot obtain leasing arrangements for second-hand equipment.

If cost-efficiency is your priority, it is possible to locate good value equipment at various office furniture and equipment auctions or other second-hand stores. As you do so, you need to bear in mind the cost of your time being expended on searching for bargains. Every hour you spend away from your practice you cannot earn income; thus you must take into account the cost of lost opportunity of earning when deciding on how to finance your initial set-up. To balance such a pure economic and rational view of the world, it is conceivable that you make a considered choice to spend more of your time in the initial stages of your business on setting it up rather than earning.

Table 3.3 *Practice ongoing cost items: A sample list*

Utilities • Water • Gas and fuel • Electricity • Rates	**Communication Systems** • Paging services • Telephone • Mobile phone
Professional development • Seminars/conferences • Travel • Memberships	**Insurances** • Professional indemnity • Public liability • Income replacement
Office • Lease • Security surveillance system • Cleaning • Maintenance	**Marketing/Advertising** • *Yellow Pages* • Client newsletters • Advertisements
Printing	**Postage/Courier**
Stationery	**Motor vehicle**
Entertainment/Food • Staff amenities • Lunches/entertainment	**Staff costs** • Salaries and wages • Superannuation • Workers' compensation

To undertake a more in-depth analysis of your expenditure you may choose to group it into fixed and variable cost categories. If there is a need to adjust or reduce expenditure, the variable costs are easier to reduce and should be targeted first. At the same time it is easier to estimate budgets when more of the costs are fixed; so whenever possible you may consider alternatives of funding items that attract variable costs.

The attitude to the start-up sum is critical here. Most businesses fail — and many fail — through undercapitalisation. Many other businesses fail for want of investment time and enterprise. The balance to be maintained is between firm containment of expenses and appropriate investment of money. Without firm budgetary control, whatever sum there is soon gets frittered away: without imaginative investment on significant issues (such as marketing) the practice will never succeed. To this end the cash flow analysis becomes crucial.

3.5.2 Financial budgeting and analysis

Although the financial standing of the business is the ultimate measure of its viability, this point is often denied or rationalised away by business owners. Unless your practice is able to earn sufficient income to provide adequate remuneration for yourself and others, you would be better to earn income in employment.

Psychologists along with other professionals working in human services are, in most cases, inadequately prepared for the financial management demands of a business. Because it is far easier to spend time on the activities we like best and avoid those we like least, financial plans are usually not given as much attention as they should be. After all, they will provide the final evidence for your decision to proceed with the set-up or otherwise of your private practice.

The objective of financial planning is to accurately estimate how much your business activities (which are contained in your business plan marketing and resources strategies) are going to cost; and how much revenue can be generated from selling the products (as defined by your business plan's service strategy).

If you are preparing your subsequent budget after having been in practice for some time, you will be able to base your predictions on existing figures, and estimate those related to the new ideas, expansions or marketing campaigns. If this is your first attempt at planning your finances, you must be prepared for some serious guesswork. At the same time, you should be as realistic as possible, both about your ability to win new clients (i.e. earn income) and about the level of expenditure. It is far better to be conservative when estimating your financial situation, and adjust it on a regular basis as more information about your performance becomes available.

The basic financial tools are:

- balance sheet;
- profit and loss statement; and
- cash-flow projection.

Balance sheet

The *balance sheet* is a commonly accepted term, but it is not well understood. In fact, most people tend to refer to the balance sheet in their everyday conversation when they really mean profit and loss statement, which is a far easier concept to comprehend. A balance sheet is a table of your practice's total worth — a list of all your assets and liabilities. It is essentially a tool of economists and accountants for appraising the wellbeing of a company at a particular time. While the balance sheet is a vital piece of paper to them, it will probably never excite a psychologist — even one in private practice. Unlike other tools, the balance sheet is also less functional for budgeting and financial planning.

Nevertheless, it is worthwhile to understand the terms contained within the balance sheet as they will significantly impact on your practice. When you are ready to sell the business, its value will be expressed in the balance sheet. You may find it worthwhile to gain more insight from accounting books for novices (e.g. Stanley, 1993).

Table 3.4 shows a sample balance sheet. It is divided into two main parts: liabilities and assets. The liabilities are essentially funds you owe and assets are the things you own. The two sides are always in balance, hence its name.

The liabilities are:

- long-term liabilities, which are all loans such as mortgages that are long term in nature;
- current liabilities, which are all debt that you need to repay in the short term; for example, bank overdraft and all the bills that are due to be paid such as electricity; and
- capital, which includes all retained profits and value of shares if your business structure is a company.

The assets are:

- fixed assets, which include the value of assets of a long-term nature, such as buildings or motor vehicles (sometimes referred to as non-current assets);
- current assets, which include assets easily converted into cash, such as bank deposits and debts owed to you by your clients;

- intangible assets (such as goodwill), which include assets that have a value only if the business is ongoing, and usually consist of expenses incurred at the initial set-up;
- investments, which include shares in other companies and loans made to others.

Table 3.4 *A sample balance sheet*

Balance sheet for financial year: ______			
Long-term liabilities:		Fixed assets:	
Mortgage	$___	Land and buildings	$___
Other loans	$___	Motor vehicles	$___
Current liabilities:		Current assets:	
Bank overdraft	$___	Short-term deposits	$___
Trade creditors (people you owe money to)	$___	Trade debtors (people owing money to you)	$___
Provisions (e.g. for taxation)	$___	*less* provisions for doubtful debts	$___
		Cash in hand	$___
		Cash at bank	$___
		Prepaid insurances	$___
Capital:		Intangible assets:	
Issued capital (if company)	$___	Formation expenses	$___
Directors' loans	$___	Patents	$___
Retained earnings (profits you left in company)	$___		
		Investments:	
		Shares	$___
Total	$___	Total	$___

Your practice's balance sheet will be prepared by your accountant once a year (or on a more regular basis if you so request) and will provide you with a snapshot value of your net assets. The balance sheets from at least 3 years of business operation will be carefully scrutinised by a bank if you apply for a substantial bank loan, and so it is a good idea to understand the basics. You certainly do not need to know the intricacies of a balance sheet to operate a successful and profitable practice. However, it will be hard to operate a successful and profitable business without the working knowledge of the next two financial tools outlined in detail below: the profit and loss statement and cash flow projection.

Profit and loss statement

The second financial tool, the profit and loss statement, is probably the most intuitive to understand because it has an immediate impact on your hip pocket. A profit and loss statement consists of the net difference between income from professional fees (or any other sources such as investments) and expenditure, including tax. In its simplest form, it looks like Table 3.5.

Table 3.5 *A sample profit & loss statement*

Profit and loss statement for financial year: _______			
Income			
Professional fees	$___		
Other income	$___		
Total income			**$___**
Expenses			
Wages and salaries	$___		
Other expenses	$___		
Total expenses		*less*	**$___**
Gross profit (loss)			**$___**
Tax		*less*	$___
NET PROFIT (LOSS)			**$___**

Profit and loss statements for past years can be presented, along with projections for the next 3 to 5 years, to demonstrate the trend in profits (or losses).

To make this sort of projection useful for yourself, and not just the bank manager, you need to estimate the income and expenditure in a more detailed manner. In the first place, for example, you need to calculate the entire costs of initial set-up to ensure you have enough cash to purchase all the equipment, and carefully evaluate various options such as renting rooms, and purchasing second-hand or new furniture.

Cash flow projection

The most powerful tool for performing this sort of financial analysis is a cash flow projection — your third financial tool. Cash flow projection is a table showing an estimate of how much ready cash you will collect and spend in each month.

No matter how big or how small your practice is, whether this is your first business plan or whether your practice has been operating for years, once you discover the power of thorough cash flow analysis your capability to run a private practice (or any business, for that matter) will greatly increase. *If you read nothing else in this section, and even if you ignore the intricacies of the business plan altogether, it is recommended that you at least consider the simple yet essential tool of financial planning, described below*. The reason for such confidence in the cash flow analysis is that it takes the uncertainty and anxiety out of business planning. If done in sufficient detail, and with a realistic and conservative approach, you can predict where the income will come from, and how much cash you need in the bank, month by month. No more sleepless nights! It is all documented and can be adjusted each time new information becomes available about how much money you really have spent. Your practical knowledge of computer spreadsheets will make this exercise much more efficient, but it is acceptable to use a large piece of paper (preferably with preprinted financial columns) and a calculator.

The structure of a cash flow projection is not unlike the profit and loss statement, except that income and expenditure are broken down into much more detailed categories, and the figures are estimated for each month. It is most common to prepare such a table for a 12-month period (see Table 3.6).

Another useful feature that should be built into the cash flow projection is the running figure for each month, alongside your previous estimates. This provides ongoing feedback to you about the accuracy of your projection, and allows for adjustment of the next month's estimated figures.

This monthly adjustment depends on your ongoing monitoring of all expenses and income and taking time to check how your business is performing at least on a monthly basis. It also depends on the financial data being available to you. Your receipts, invoices and cheque butts must be organised in some systematic way so that the monthly financial check will not be a difficult and time-consuming task. The information systems that are vital to this task are further discussed in detail in Section 4.12. You may choose, of course, to pass this task on to your bookkeeper or accountant, but if you do so, you must keep in mind that you are the only person who has the information about the direction in which your business is heading and your capacity to generate more income.

When estimating income at the top part of Table 3.6 you can split it into as many categories as you find useful. For example, each project or each group of clients being referred from one particular source may constitute one type of income. This way you can reflect the expected income from the planned marketing campaigns included in your marketing strategy.

Remember that this table is to be a reflection of actual cash flow. That is, both income and expenditure should be entered in those months when cash is expected to come into the bank and payments are made. Some of the projects can last for an extended period of time, at the end of which you should issue an invoice for your services. The actual payment, however, may not appear until the terms of payment have

Table 3.6 *A sample cash flow*

CASH FLOW PROJECTION **FOR THE PERIOD:** ________ **Date prepared:** ________

INCOME																
SOURCE OF INCOME	July		August		September		October		April		May		June		TOTAL	
	Est.	Act.	Est.	Act.	Est.	Act.	Est.	Act.	Est.	Act.	Est.	Act.	Est.	Act.	Est.	Act.
Professional fees																
Seminars																
Compensation clients																
Private clients																
Training projects																
Subtotal																
OTHER INCOME																
TOTAL																
Progressive total																
EXPENDITURE																
Accounting fees																
Advertising/Marketing																
Bank charges																
Cleaning																
Computer software																
Courier																
Employee amenities																
Entertainment																
Fringe benefits tax (FBT)																
Heating/gas & fuel																
Insurance																
Leases																
Legal fees																
Library																
Light & power																
Vehicle expenses																
Office security																
Postage																
Printing																
Rates																
Rent — office																
Repairs & maintenance																
Office equipment																
Stationery																
Superannuation																
Telephone																
Training																
Travel & accommodation																
Wages & tax																
WorkCover																
TOTAL																
SURPLUS (DEFICIT)																
Bank balance																

expired, and in many cases much later (this issue of managing debt is further discussed in Section 4.10.2). Conversely, when you receive bills from your suppliers you usually have a few weeks in which to pay. The payments and receipts of cash are entered in the cash flow projection table in the month in which they are expected to be paid.

The bottom part of Table 3.6 consists of expenditure items, also divided into as many categories as seems appropriate to provide sufficient detail for planning. These categories ideally should correspond to the 'accounts', used by your accountant to analyse your final end-of-year profit and loss statement for taxation purposes. They can be even more detailed so that the actual analysis immediately makes sense to you. For example, if you have a number of leases, you can separate each lease payment.

3.5.3 Obtaining a loan

It is possible to develop a successful psychology practice with very little capital investment, mainly because the business of psychology is neither stock nor equipment intensive. Further, the success in this, sometimes colloquially referred to as 'brain business', has far more to do with the skills and capability of the practitioner than the amount of capital investment in marble offices and glossy brochures.

At the same time, the oft committed error of most businesses is undercapitalisation; that is, spending too little at the set-up stage and therefore reducing the potential profit that is linked to return on investment. To balance the small capital outlay, most practitioners expend vast amounts of time, which is in many instances a reasonable approach in the absence of easily available funds.

It is likely that, at some stage of your practice development, you will recognise the need for funding your plans to generate more business. The most accessible business funding is in the form of a bank overdraft. This usually requires some security such as a mortgage over your family home to the amount equal to the required overdraft. It is similar to a credit facility, and not unlike a credit card, except that the amounts involved are as large as you can convince the bank manager you can safely repay.

This is where your business plan becomes essential. It is hard to portray a confident and business-like image without a document that can demonstrate you have seriously considered your business opportunities and prepared appropriate strategies. It is far better to present the plan at the first meeting with the bank manager. Your accountant will also advise you with respect to the availability of various funding options and their requirements. The business plan does not have to be a long and wordy document. In fact, the more concise the better, but it must include a financial analysis such as cash flow projection. You should not be surprised if a bank representative immediately turns to this section and works backwards from it, asking some pertinent questions about the validity of your optimism regarding the generation of income from clients about whom the bank has very little knowledge.

Once your line of credit is established, it is likely that your financial performance will be reviewed on a regular basis, which may involve forwarding your end-of-year financial statements and/or taxation returns to the bank. Most banks will charge you interest only when you use the overdraft, but there are some banks that still charge the establishment fee and ongoing fee for the privilege of having a line of credit (for example, 1% of the total overdraft amount per year) irrespective of whether you use it or not. It pays to do some shopping to find the best deal, particularly with the current competitive environment in the financial service sector.

As an alternative to bank overdrafts, you may consider short-term leasing or hire-purchase arrangements. It is quite probable that most of the initial set-up funds will be needed for equipment, such as office furniture, computer, photocopier or facsimile. As long as you are prepared to give personal guarantees and your credit history is not problematic you will find it quite easy to make a lease arrangement, usually for 4 years, with some residual (e.g. 20–40%) to be repaid at the end of the lease period. At that stage you may be ready to trade in the old equipment and take out another lease.

Under a lease arrangement, the equipment remains the property of the finance company; thus all the payments are tax deductible. Under a hire-purchase arrangement you become the owner of the purchased goods, in which case they will appear as fixed assets in your balance sheet. Their depreciation (which ranges from 15% to 30% depending on the type of equipment), as well as the interest paid to the financial institution, are tax deductible.

3.5.4 Wealth creation

While you are planning the financial aspects of your business it is easy to forget that you should also be planning your own financial future. You are an independent entity from your business, although it may sometimes be difficult to separate the two. The initial 'honeymoon' period of private practice often gives way to a desire to 'have something to show for all my hard work' other than overdrafts, loans and a tired family. To prevent such physical, emotional and professional exhaustion, it is recommended that you consider your own financial future and view your business venture as part of your personal wealth creation and a path to financial independence. Rather than viewing your practice as something that drives you, perhaps a healthier approach might be to use it as a tool to achieve your personal goals.

Start with your own goals and personal mission — a topic of many worthwhile books (Covey, 1993). Once you have these clearly worked out you will know the level of finances required. The structure and financial plan of your business should reflect these goals. For example, if your needs for ready cash are mainly long term you will be wise to plan for substantial superannuation contributions as part of your own wealth creation. Although constantly changing, the superannuation system is still one of the most tax-effective ways to save for the future. You might even consider starting your own superannuation fund, with some assistance from your accountant and financial adviser, which can then provide your practice with funds to purchase equipment and/or building.

It will be appreciated that having a private practice or a business is rarely an end in itself but is, rather, a significant part of a larger life picture. Among the functions of a private practice are the creation of an income; the development of a worthwhile economic asset; the development of a lifestyle that gives considerable autonomy; and an involvement in an enterprise that you regard as significantly worthwhile.

Within that context the financial and aspirational aspects are intertwined. Having a successful business not only keeps you financially successful and gives a sense of worth, but also develops as something that you own, and can eventually sell if you wish. Part of your planning may be to develop a business that you can sell to do something different, or use the proceeds to eventually retire.

During the course of your career benefits may arise that were not foreseen. For example, what you do may be so innovative as to result in the development of a psychological test for which you own the copyright. Other benefits may be to develop a course that you can franchise, write a book that significantly enhances your professional reputation, franchise your practice or provide a unique service.

Later in his life the novelist A. J. Cronin wrote a book called *Adventures in Two Worlds*. The general thrust of what he had to say is that in one's youth the material and the technological hold sway. As one gets older the intangible world of values becomes progressively more dominant. These two worlds are, in other words, of different salience at different times of life.

A business must be financially successful if it is to be regarded as successful — but not financially successful at any price. Thus the intangibles become increasingly important as your career progresses. Later in a career few would want to reflect that they made it successful by trampling on others and by shady behaviour. The goodwill that an ethical practice demonstrates is convertible to cash on sale. Attention to cash flow, and attention to wealth creation by innovation and hard work, go hand in hand with close attention to professional values.

In a rural community your plan may be to make available a service formerly denied those living in remote communities. It is this use of creative intelligence, combined with hard work, that makes for really successful enterprises. To succeed at a higher level there is a need to work smarter rather than harder, and this is often helped by an interchange of ideas with a creative and discreet colleague.

Your long-term personal aim should be building wealth; otherwise, you may find that a lot of money has slipped through your hands over the many years you have been in private practice. Some helpful advice can be obtained from financial planners and investment specialists. Exercise caution, particularly when the advice given is not on a fee-for-service basis. When the financial planner gains income from a commission from certain investment funds, it is not hard to imagine which ones they will recommend. Always find out how the income of your adviser is derived.

3.5.5 Estate planning

Estate planning is even more long term and has to do with what happens after you have left the practice or have died. It is important to consider your will and the way your dependants will be looked after, as well as how your business will be managed in your absence. The need for a current will applies to anyone, but particularly to someone operating a business under a complex structure. Your will should be up to date and reviewed regularly to ensure that it reflects your intentions.

You should also establish an enduring power of attorney — which means that you will appoint another person to act on your behalf in financial and personal matters in a situation where you are unable to act for yourself whether for geographical or medical reasons.

You may also consider testamentary trust wills. These establish a discretionary trust for each of the beneficiaries who can benefit under the will. The primary beneficiary then has a number of options for his or her share of the estate, for example:

- Take all or part of the capital immediately or at any time during the remainder of his or her life.
- Distribute income from year to year to relatives of his or her choice.
- Take a capital loan from the trust without interest.

Another advantage of a testamentary trust is that it is protected against insolvency of a beneficiary. It also protects pension entitlements.

When creating your will you must consider who will control the business in the future: how you would like the management succession to take place, and what roles various people should play in your absence. It makes sense, of course, to talk to them first about your plans.

It is always advisable to seek professional assistance when you are unsure of what to do. In this case, your solicitor should be asked for advice.

4
Establishing your practice

So far, you will have completed a soul-searching exercise as to whether you are ready to enter the business world, chosen the area of your practice and prepared a business plan. The time has now come to begin the practice. You will need to make some basic decisions about such things as the physical setting and your stationery. Think of yourself as a project manager or a co-ordinator of numerous set-up activities, such as printing, selecting equipment, identifying options for a telephone system, negotiating with insurance salespeople, and the like.

If you are the sort of person who dislikes this sort of administrative activity it might be better to seek someone's assistance. Since you are the one who will be the principal behind the practice, it will pay to spend some time on these mundane issues and work through the pain. This stage will pass as you become established and most of the decisions are made and tasks undertaken, and they will not have to be faced again. As you upgrade your telephone or computer systems, increase your premises, review your stationery and so on, you will be able to improve the practice and correct some of the errors made in the initial set-up stage. Your becoming business 'street-wise' at this early stage will have many advantages in the future.

4.1 Choosing your practice name

The name of your practice, in most cases, will be the name of the company, trust or a registered business name. If the business structure you have chosen is a sole operator using your own name, this decision will be quite simple.

It may be of interest to note that even though your business name or company name has been selected, this structure can still trade under another name that is more appropriate for the marketplace. An example is ABC-XYZ Nominees Pty Ltd trading as 'People Professionals', where the trading name is displayed more prominently. If you would like to choose this option, you will need to register the trading name with the appropriate State Corporate Affairs body, as you would with any other business name (see Section 3.3). As mentioned before, if you would like to use the word 'Psychology' or any derivative of it, some psychologists registration boards require that you seek their approval.

In selecting the name of your practice, the guiding thought should be the perception of your target market. Beside giving you a sense of identity, it must also send an effective message to those with whom you want to do business. For example, if your target group consists of lawyers, it would be worthwhile to design the sort of name that communicates a sense of prestige and credibility, not unlike a name associated with a solicitors' firm, for example 'Menzies and Associates'. If your selected market comprises chief executives of large companies, your practice name should convey a corporate image, for example 'IPC Corporate Solutions'.

One way to identify a suitable name is to search through the currently registered names or even the relevant sections of the *Yellow Pages*: Training and Development, Psychologists, Management Consultants, and such like. You will discover, for example, that names of many corporations tend to consist of three-letter acronyms, such as IBM, CBA, CRA or BHP, and it is easy to convey this image with a similar 'code'.

To check if your perception matches that of your target market group it is recommended that you perform a 'pilot test' on a selected and representative sample. Here is another example of where you can put your hard-earned psychological research skills to good use. They will give you a competitive advantage over businesses managed by people without such skills. The idea of pilot testing is applicable to any other activities involving communication with a target audience, for example in marketing.

While it is easy to expend a lot of effort, time and money on selecting the name and testing its acceptance in the marketplace, this task should be seen in its proper perspective. Your practice name is important in that it immediately communicates a message; however, the service you provide and how you provide it will, in most instances, overshadow any effect of the name. There are many stories of psychologists, and other professionals in private practice, who had hired business name and design experts, only to end up with a name such as 'Surname Psychology Services' or 'Surname Corporate Psychology'.

4.2 Designing a logo

Following the decision on the practice name, the dilemma of designing an appropriate logo for the business usually appears, calling for some creative flair. As with the selection of the name, there is a danger of investing a disproportionate amount of time and resources into this task.

It is best to commence the process with a clear list of descriptors and characteristics of your practice. You may, for example, describe your business in terms of the feelings you would like to generate in the person dealing with you. Should it have a corporate image, or a soft and warm feeling? What sort of first impression would you like to create in someone looking at your logo?

Many companies take their business logo very seriously as it identifies their public image. Sometimes they change it in line with a new public image they would like to create. Such public changes have been recently observed in Telstra and the Commonwealth Bank of Australia. It is interesting to note that, after much discussion and design creation, quite simple images usually appear.

A lesson to be learned from observing others go through the process of logo design is that the simpler and clearer the image, the better. It does not matter if it is abstract, since people will use their own 'ink blot test' to interpret it, in any case. If it produces the sort of meaning and image you would like to create in your audience it has fulfilled its purpose.

To prevent others utilising it, you may register your business logo as a patent or trademark. Your solicitor will advise on you on the process and cost involved.

4.3 Designing and printing stationery

Once your practice has a name, and possibly a logo, it has an identity. The next step is to demonstrate its identity to the world around you. This is first done by printing business stationery, which includes business cards, letterhead, compliments slips and envelopes.

4.3.1 Business cards

The normally accepted custom is that you authenticate your identity through your business card. The business card communicates your status within the business entity, as well as your professional standing. As a minimum, a business card should contain:

- business trading name and its logo, if applicable;
- your full name;
- your title within the business entity (e.g. Consultant, Counselling Psychologist);
- your qualifications;
- business address;

- telephone numbers on which you would like your clients to contact you (e.g. business, mobile, home);
- fax number;
- pager number;
- electronic mail address (e-mail, which is discussed in more detail in Section 4.6.9).

It is your responsibility to make sure that you are legally permitted to use the title you include on all stationery, including your business card. That is, your title has to be consistent with that registered by the relevant registration board. Registration boards require you to be a 'psychologist'. Only if they recognise you as a designated specialist should you use a specialist title.

If your practice involves making appointments with clients, you may consider including appointment times on the reverse side of your business card. Space for the time of the next appointment could be provided; for example, 'Your next appointment is: Date:________ Time:________'.

In offices where a number of professionals practise you will usually find small display stands containing all the relevant business cards. You may consider placing your cards on the reception counter so that your clients reporting to the reception or any other potential clients can take one.

Some practitioners have chosen to design and print their own stationery, given the easy and relatively cheap access to desktop publishing software, computers and high-quality printers such as laser (discussed in more detail in Section 4.12.3). Here is a word of warning: while it is possible to design a relatively high-quality letterhead and print it directly on the laser printer with each letter or invoice, this is not the case with the business card. One reason for this is the thickness of the paper stock on which business cards are normally printed, which a standard laser printer will not handle. Second, you will need to cut printed paper into the required number of cards, making straight edges with even margins rather difficult to achieve, even with a paper guillotine. The resultant image left with the client is that the business is not able to afford real business cards. While producing one's own cards may be quite appropriate for a business involved in creative arts and cottage industry, such as pottery, it is not the norm among professional service providers.

4.3.2 Business letterheads

Along with the business card, you will also need to design a matching letterhead so that your practice can establish an official contact with the outside world through letters, invoices and reports.

If your practice is trading under an incorporated structure, such as a limited company or a trustee company, there are special legal requirements for displaying the following on the letterhead:

- the business trading name (if different from the full name of the company);
- the full name of the company including 'Proprietary', 'Pty', 'Limited' or 'Ltd' (as appropriate);
- the company's ACN (Australian Company Number) — every Australian company, proprietary or stock exchange listed, has one of these unique numbers.

In addition to these legal requirements you will also wish to include the following on your letterhead:

- practice address or addresses, if there is more than one, in which case you may like to indicate to which address correspondence should be addressed;
- telephone number, usually the main office/clinic contact; and
- facsimile number.

If your practice trades under a registered business name, the name and the ACN must be displayed on letterheads, invoices, receipts, written orders and written demands for payment.

You may wish to print invoice stationery that specifically includes the invoice-related details. It is acceptable within the professional service business world to use your letterheads for this purpose, with the added word 'Invoice' prominently placed somewhere on the page.

As with business cards (see Section 4.3.1), it is possible to produce reasonable quality letterheads using home/office computer technology. Your scanned logo together with practice name, address and telephone numbers can be printed from a template every time the contents of a letter or report are produced. This assumes the use of either a laser or, at least, an ink-jet printer. The advantage of such a course of action is that you do not have to spend extra on large numbers of preprinted letterheads.

The disadvantages of printing one's own letterhead are the loss of quality, limitation to black print and the need to print every time you want to use a letterhead, even for handwritten material. While this approach may be quite reasonable for invoices, you need to consider again the sort of image you would like your private practice to project into its market. If your recognised value is to be low-cost and self-sufficiency, this would be an effective way of demonstrating your commitment to such values. It may be appropriate, for low-income clients or community non-profit organisations, but it may not be a desirable message in the corporate sector.

The reason for higher expectations of printed quality is that personal computers have raised the standards for everyone. This means that a high school student is able to produce a good-quality report quite cheaply.

The corporate world, at the same time, because of its competitive paradigm, needs to distinguish between its different levels of commitment to quality.

In addition to the quality of print, your image will also be projected through the stock on which your letterhead is printed: its thickness and type, the number of colours used and the overall design. While it is important to reiterate that there is far more to running a successful practice than image creation, it pays to be mindful of the perceptions generated in the client via symbols embedded into the business and professional service culture. If funds are your foremost consideration, the cost of the stationery design can well be minimised without greatly compromising your practice standing. As you consider investing more money into the business you may consider all the seemingly small impressions that can yield big impacts.

4.3.3 Envelopes

It is standard to display your private practice name, logo and postal address on the outside of an envelope, usually on the left-hand top corner.

The address you choose to place on the envelope should be your preferred postal address. If you practise from a number of clinics or offices, this address will correspond to the one from which your practice is being administered. If you have a post office box or a special postal bag arrangement, you may choose to limit this information to the postal address. Telephone numbers do not appear on the envelope.

4.3.4 Compliments slips

Compliments slips are pieces of paper, usually a third of an A4 page in size or even smaller. They also contain your practice name, logo, address and contact details. The words ‘With compliments’ are printed somewhere near the top.

These slips are attached to various items that you forward via post or courier, and may contain short handwritten messages. Often the slips are simply attached to a relevant document to signify that its origin was your practice, without any writing.

If the resources that you have earmarked for spending on stationery design and printing are very limited, the compliments slips can be omitted and letterhead used for those infrequent occasions when a handwritten note is necessary.

4.3.5 Fax headers

If you plan to use a facsimile machine (see Section 4.6.8 for more discussion on fax communication), you will find it useful to design a fax header sheet that identifies you and the recipient. This can be used for typing or handwriting a message to the recipient. Fax header sheets are used as the first page of an outgoing fax to easily identify both the sender and the recipient.

Give some thought to the design of your fax header sheet, to enable it to be easily identified with your practice, particularly if you use fax communication on a frequent basis. It should include at least:

- your name;
- the practice name, address, and phone and fax numbers;
- the number of pages being transmitted (clearly stating whether the header sheet is included in the total count); and
- the recipient's name, and phone and fax numbers.

Because the quality of anything transmitted by fax is drastically reduced by the process of faxing, there is little point in obtaining high-quality fax headers through commercial printing process. Computer printing in this instance is quite satisfactory.

4.4 Choosing the venue

4.4.1 What's in an address?

The above discussion of printing stationery has introduced the notion of an image of private practice, its projection and importance. It is probably true to say that anything a business does in its communication with the public, and therefore with its clients, contributes to its overall image. The message of the business's values are communicated at times very subtly, and often more powerfully than a business owner is prepared to admit. One of those not so subtle messages is embedded within the practice address.

The authors' anecdotal evidence suggests that when unsolicited material arrives on a potential client's or referrer's desk, the first question tends to be: 'Do I know this person or this company?'. If the answer is 'No', and your material still has the reader's interest, the next quick check is the address. The type of address that has the least trust and attraction is a post office box number without a street address.

The venue from which your private practice operates sends a powerful message about yourself, your values and your status as a provider of professional services. It is recommended that you choose it wisely. If financial imperatives prevent you from renting professional premises on a full-time basis, you may consider a sessional basis or a staged process of beginning at home with the aim of moving when client referrals or projects increase to sufficiently high levels.

4.4.2 The joys and pitfalls of a home-based practice

While some counselling and clinical psychologists currently operate their practices from home, the appropriateness of home as a counselling clinic has been questioned for decades (e.g. Whitta, 1969; White & Sarfaty, 1970). The arguments against using your home centre upon the undermining of the professional image of psychology, and the safety risk to which all household occupants are exposed.

The more important consideration appears to be that relating to the issue of professionalism of psychology. In recent years more small businesses than ever before operate from home because of the progress in computer and telecommunications technology. This change has not been observed among professionals dealing with the public in relationships essentially based on professional trust. Thus, there are very few medical practitioners or lawyers practising from home.

The most important factor to consider in choosing the location for your practice is the effect it will have on potential and existing clients. It may be, for example, quite appropriate for an educational psychologist to provide a service for students at home, as they are likely to expect a similar locale for other professionals servicing them (e.g. music teachers). Organisational clients, on the other hand, will expect that their employees will be hosted in a professional office when they are referred for a selection assessment. You will get most attention from readers of your brochures if you are in a well-recognised suburb such as a central business district or an inner suburb with an established name for medical or business offices.

Clients seeking personal psychological assistance will probably accept a home-clinic without complaining unless their expectations have been previously heightened by other professional clinic standards. Even then, because of the nature of the relationship, they are unlikely to express their surprise about, or dissatisfaction with, the quality of the premises of the psychologist.

It is important also to consider that the fees you charge (as will be discussed in more detail in Section 4.9) are linked to your client's perception of the intrinsic value of your services. Thus, if you practise from a suburban home-office, it would be normally expected that your practice's savings on commercial office rent would be reflected in your fees, particularly if your clients are expected to call at your practice.

As a reader planning to practise from home you may well form an argument for a home-based office/practice on the basis of the recent trends of Small Office Home Office (SOHO). Such trends can be observed, for example, through the rapid growth of the association supporting this industry sector. A similar trend that has also been predicted, although it has not eventuated with the same speed, is the increase in people telecommuting to work, that is, working from home using modem connections to their main office computer in the city. It needs to be remembered that such home-based businesses are rarely operating as professional or consulting rooms dealing with the public.

In the light of such trends in the Australian workscape, it should be noted that it may be quite appropriate for some professionals to operate a successful private practice from home. An example could be an organisational psychologist, most of whose work is conducted on the client's premises or at hired training venues. In a situation where financial resources are limited, quite a valid decision may be to save on office lease, and invest instead in technology such as computers, software or presentation tools. The gains from such investments are likely to outweigh the disadvantages associated with working from home, at least in the short term.

On the positive side, there are some advantages of working from home. One of the more obvious ones is reduced travel time, as long as this saving in time is spent on other productive activities. Proximity to your cohabitants and the flexibility of being able to engage in home activities while you are not involved in practice work can be both positive and negative, depending on your personal situation. A financial advantage is that you may be able to offset the increased costs of electricity, heating and telephone against the business. If you are planning to do so for an extended period of time you will need to seek advice from your accountant. There may, however, be capital gains tax implications if your home is used for income-earning purposes and you plan to sell it. If you claim only consumables (proportion of heating, light, phone and so on) it should not affect the tax during the time before the sale of your family home. If you start costing the premises, seek an accountant's advice. At the same time, you will need to weigh up the disadvantage associated with isolation when working on your own at home.

4.4.3 Sharing professional rooms

There are a number of alternatives for the practice location, other than your own home, which are economical and offer a more professional image. One of these is sharing a clinic or office with another professional. Such an arrangement can be either on a sessional basis or for an agreed regular period. Sessional basis means that you only pay for the rooms when you actually use them, usually when you see a client or need to use facilities. The other payment basis involves a regular rent per week or month, for an agreed number of days, irrespective of whether you use the office or not. While the former option is usually more expensive per hour, it may be more cost effective if the number of clients you see is low and unpredictable.

As previously mentioned, the type of professionals with whom you could share a room will depend on the area of psychology you specialise in, and it is expected that their premises will in some way resemble the type that your clientele will find attractive and appropriate.

If you wish to share but do not have any personal helpful contacts and cannot locate relevant advertisements in the local papers, you may choose simply to call in and introduce yourself to the owner. You may find that often such professionals are keen to negotiate a rent deal to mutual satisfaction, especially when they have one or more rooms vacant on their property.

One advantage of such an arrangement with an established office or clinic is that it usually has staffed reception areas, whose services can also be negotiated as part of the overall rental. This becomes one of the most significant issues when attempting to operate a practice, initially with no full-time staff to manage the in-coming calls — a fundamental activity for a business constantly dealing with people and appointments (This is further discussed in Section 4.6.) Depending on the extent of the reception and administrative assistance you receive at the shared premises, it can be referred to as a version of a 'serviced office' arrangement.

Thus, when working out how much is reasonable for accommodation, you need to take into account all the costs of the reception, salaries, communication systems and telephones (see Chapter 3). Once you know how much these would cost if you were to set up your own premises, you may then be willing to pay more when renting premises with extra reception facilities. Conversely, you will also have a basis on which to argue that the rental is too expensive.

4.4.4 Renting serviced offices

Serviced offices are becoming increasingly available in major cities in response to a greater number of consulting professionals of all kinds who practise on their own. The target clientele for such service businesses are those professionals who recognise the need for a better address than a home office, and who cannot afford full-time staff to fulfil their administrative needs.

In a serviced office arrangement you rent one or more fully furnished rooms for an agreed weekly amount and utilise all the available facilities at an extra charge on a user-pays basis. This usually includes use of boardroom, typing, facsimile, photocopying and computer. You have an allocated telephone number and it is answered in your practice name, as per agreed instructions. Your telephone messages and your mail are also stored for you, and other normal administrative support is provided.

Serviced offices vary from highest quality office buildings in the central business district through to smaller places in outer suburbs. Their advertisements can usually be found in newspapers since the turnover of their clients is relatively high. Some serviced offices provide a very low price entry into such an arrangement, from say $65 per week, for the right to their address on your letterhead, your phone answered in your practice's name, basic mail-holding facility and 1 hour's use of the office cubicle, not unlike one you may be familiar with in a library.

The more reputable serviced offices usually have reciprocal arrangements in other capital cities. This means that if you rent an office in one city, you have a right to use similar offices in other states, and in some cases to use all their interstate addresses on your letterhead.

This option will most likely appeal to an organisational or vocational psychologist who needs to portray an appropriate image to corporate clients. Counselling and clinical psychologists need to ensure that their clients' calls are dealt with appropriately by making appointments for you to see them. This is less likely to be achieved by a serviced office receptionist whose main role and training is usually limited to taking messages for you to return your calls. Some training may be necessary.

4.4.5 Leasing independent office space

Another practice location option is to lease independent office space. You need to be ready to make this move as far as your business development is concerned because it will have obvious risks attached. First, the immediate rental cost and the ongoing nature of your liability for such payments have to be considered. The lease period usually lasts from a minimum of 2 years to 5 years. Lease contracts usually include penalties if you wish to cancel before the expiry date, at least for the owner's cost of finding another tenant. For this and other reasons it is recommended that you seek the advice of your solicitor before signing the contract, as you would with any binding legal agreement. Minimise your risks, and make yourself fully aware of all the implications of your decision.

Additional costs in the initial outlay category that are associated with renting your premises include its full furnishing and partitioning, unless such items already exist on the premises. While office partitioning can cost around $300 per linear metre, it is usually left behind by most tenants as it is cheaper to build these than to shift them. One of the distinguishing features of offices required by psychologists is the need for enclosed offices for each professional in order to create a confidential atmosphere. Thus, the required office space per practitioner is usually more than the equivalent for other offices for which open floor plan is adequate.

As a rough estimate each single office requires a minimum of 14 square metres (150 square feet). When you add reception, administration, waiting and kitchen areas to your estimates, it is possible to operate a comfortable practice for one practitioner from around 45 square metres (500 square feet). With more practitioners this will reduce via shared reception, kitchen, and so on. The area you require is important because the rental prices are usually expressed in terms of cost per square unit (metre or foot) per annum. Hence, in newspaper advertisements (usually hidden in the 'Business' sections of daily papers as opposed to 'Real Estate' sections), you will often see a reference to 'office space', its area and price with little further information. The prices, to provide as a basis for the estimate of your expenditure, can be around $80 to $300 per square metre per year ($8 to $30 per square foot). This will vary according to the quality and location of the building, and the overall current demand and supply ratios of office space in the particular city.

In addition to the agreed rental amount you can also expect to pay for 'outgoings', which include rates, water, electricity and other such utilities, which can add $30 to $80 per square metre ($3 to $8 per square foot) per year to the overall cost. Parking can also add more costs to the equation, particularly if the office is in an identified business district. Parking prices can cost up to $350 per calendar month per car space.

In estimating your budgets and your ability to afford rented premises, as a general rule its cost should not exceed 5% of your practice's annual income. When deciding on the option of practice premises you need to take into account not just the current income but the projected income according to your service, marketing and financial strategies. You need to be guided to some extent by your vision of where you would like your business to be and what sort of clients you would like to service. Then your behaviour needs to reflect this vision, including where and how you receive your clients.

Operating a business from leased offices will also call for independent staffing of at least the reception area. The person performing this function can also be responsible for administration of the practice.

4.4.6 Owning an office building

Another even more expensive option, in the short term, is owning your own building. When you account for all the rental costs over a number of years, it may occur to you that there are parallels in your renting or owning a residential property. Most people opt for purchasing their home, because of the long-term gains. A main difference between owning a home and an office/clinic is its location.

The location of such a building and its appropriateness for your practice should be the overriding criteria for such a decision, but the investment potential and its value should also be considered. This is important, especially if you plan for your practice to expand in size and therefore increase in the required office or clinic area. If the building you purchase becomes too small to house your practice, its location needs to lend itself to being readily rented out to someone else. In other words, you need to see this option as a long-term investment and a wealth-creation strategy at the same time as a practice-development strategy. If you were to select this option you need to be comfortable with becoming a landlord/landlady and all that this responsibility entails.

The main advantages of owning a building from which you practise is that you receive, as the landlord/landlady, income from the practice income. The two practical ways of achieving this objective, with little extra cash are, first, through a loan secured against equity in your home (or some other investment); and, second, through the use of your superannuation fund (see the discussion on wealth creation in Section 3.5.4).

The superannuation option assumes that you operate your own fund which, when properly structured, can purchase and rent a building to your practice at commercial rates. The difficulty you need to overcome in this scenario is that a superannuation fund cannot borrow money. Your accountant would need to advise you on the available options that may include the set-up of a special trust which can issue units to the fund. Further, investment decisions must be conducted at arm's length from your practice needs, always aiming to achieve the maximum benefit of superannuation fund members (that is yourself and your family members) rather than your business.

This option is obviously quite complex and you would be well advised to seek opinion and assistance from suitably qualified professionals. It is presented here simply as a demonstration of one of many innovative ways to locate premises of high quality that can be either done very economically or with long-term investment as an outcome.

4.5 Insurances

A fundamental task you need to undertake prior to the commencement of your practice is to take out insurances that will provide the necessary cover in case of any adverse and unforeseen circumstances. As a minimum, you should have the following current insurance policies at any time during the operation of your practice:

- professional indemnity;
- public liability; and
- fire and theft for your practice premises.

It is important to note that if you operate your practice from home, your home insurance may not cover the area and the items used for income generation, as they would normally attract a commercial rate. It is recommended to seek advice from an insurance broker regarding the above vital insurance policies. A broker can usually obtain the least expensive rate for your insurance needs.

Professional indemnity insurance is very competitively provided by the insurance firm providing a policy package for members of the Australian Psychological Society. Non-members may also obtain insurance from Minet, which provides the excellent deal to APS members, but at a higher premium. Other major insurance companies also provide professional indemnity insurance for psychologists.

In the area of personal insurance needs you also should consider the levels of your current policy cover for:

- life insurance;
- income protection; and
- disability cover.

When your income is totally dependent on your capacity to work, and when you are no longer protected by an employer's sick leave provisions, it is up to you to insure your income ability. You will need to weigh up your personal situation, taking into account the level of debt you are exposed to, your personal and family needs, and the period of time you can survive with no income; and consider the cost of each insurance. In this area your financial adviser may be the best source of assistance.

You may also consider joining a health fund. A severe illness — even if brief — could erode your capital and put the business at risk.

4.6 Communication systems

Irrespective of what sort of premises you choose for your practice, you will need to address its communication systems. These comprise the means by which your clients will be able to contact you, and how and when you will return their calls if you are unavailable. In particular, if your practice depends on seeing clients face to face in a counselling-type contact, the question you need to clearly answer is: 'What process will my potential clients go through to make appointments with me?'.

While it is acceptable in a corporate world to place calls to a professional who is not always available, leave the message and have the call returned, it is not the case with members of the general public who wish to make appointments with a professional. Their expectation is that the process of booking an appointment will be relatively painless.

For a general public client and for a corporate-type client (which includes referrers of clients) you need to establish foolproof systems of communication. The authors are intimately aware of a significant gap in this fundamental area of business conduct of many psychologists (from their personal attempts to systematically contact groups of practising colleagues). The phone numbers used were those provided by practitioners as their business contact numbers. If psychology as a profession is to improve its standing in the community, this area, more than any other, needs to dramatically improve in the next decade.

No business can operate in isolation from the outside world, particularly a business that provides services to the public. Some large corporations have estimated, as part of their risk management exercise, that they would be out of business within days if their telephone systems suddenly stopped functioning. This is just as true of professional service business.

There is more to effective communication systems built into a successful business than listing a telephone number on which the practitioner is sometimes available. The aim is to achieve the highest quality of each transaction between your practice and the client or anyone who chooses to contact your practice, for that matter. In designing communication solutions for your business you may wish to consider the following checklist of questions that will most likely be processed by your clients, even if quite unconsciously:

- How long does it take for the phone to be answered?
- How is the phone answered — does it seem professional?
- Does the receptionist clearly identify the practice?
- Is the receptionist's manner warm and courteous?
- Are clients' queries handled to their satisfaction?
- Are clients given immediate options if the person they phoned (most likely yourself) is unavailable?
- How long does it take for clients' calls to be returned?
- How many times is the phone engaged when clients phone?

In this era of communication revolution there are many cost-effective and readily available options particularly geared for small business. The choices explored below assume that you do not employ someone whose sole responsibility is to answer the phones and that you are a sole practitioner in the initial practice set-up phase. It is further assumed that you cannot answer all the calls yourself since you would be either engaged on other calls or with clients.

4.6.1 Call waiting systems

One of the simplest ways in which to overcome the problem of an engaged phone is to install an Easycall™ system, with a call waiting and a call diversion facility, currently offered by Telstra. To find out more, simply contact the company providing your telephone services. As long as the exchange in your area has such capabilities, and you have a touch phone, it is usually only a matter of requesting the extra service (it may even be free). It does not involve any extra cable connections. The way this dual line operates is that when another caller dials your line while you are engaged in another telephone conversation, you can hear a distinct beeping tone. You can either ask the first caller to wait or terminate the call. Then, by pressing appropriate designated buttons on your touch phone, you connect with the second caller.

One of the disadvantages of this system is that you have only a limited time (of the order of six rings) before the second call becomes unavailable to you, and as far as that caller is concerned you did not answer the call. This is probably the worst scenario in the business customer relations sense. For, when your phone is engaged the potential clients may give you another chance and try again if they really want to reach you, but when it seems that you do not answer your phone at all, the message is as good as: 'I am out of business'. Furthermore, while this option may solve the problem of the engaged phone, it does nothing to help you communicate with your clients while you are busy with other business activities. You will need other technology to assist with this common problem of a small professional practice.

4.6.2 Telephone answering machines

The simplest and least effective way to deal with the problem of the sole practitioner's unavailability is a telephone answering machine. Despite the penetration of answering machines into the marketplace, there are many people who react with some anxiety when they need to record their message on tape. It seems logical that this problem will be more frequently experienced by the specific target group of psychologists' clients in a clinical or a counselling setting. Intuitively, it would seem that clients who phone to make an appointment for a problem of a psychological nature are not likely to leave a coherent message on an answering machine. They will also, understandably, not want to leave a spoken record for non-professionals (receptionists), and they might not be prepared to leave their name and phone number without an assurance of confidentiality.

If you do choose to include an answering machine within your business communication system it is useful to select one that enables you to listen to messages remotely. You do this by simply dialling your own number and then dialling a personal identification number when your greeting is heard. Most telephones now utilise a pulse dial exchange technology, which means that you need to press telephone buttons to send the secret code to your answering machine. If the telephone you are using to remotely obtain your messages does not have such capability, you can purchase a small numerical pad that will enable message retrieval from any phone. This is especially useful when travelling in remote locations, and when using public phones to check your messages. Most answering machines can also inform you whether or not any messages have been recorded, by the number of rings they take to answer, which means that you actually pay for the long distance call only when you can be sure that a message has been recorded.

When you record your greeting on the answering machine you need to consider the listener's perceptions. Your greeting needs to encourage that person to leave a message rather than hang up, and so it needs to be friendly but professional at the same time. The message should not be too long, or long distance and mobile callers may get frustrated at the wasted cost of their call. The usually accepted form of a greeting message includes these components:

- introduction of the practice name;
- a short apology for not being personally available;
- encouragement and reminder to leave the caller's name and phone number;
- a short statement of commitment that the call will be returned; and
- a quick reassurance that the caller is important to you.

It may also pay to monitor how your greeting message is received by the callers. It is often possible to note how many callers had hung up without leaving a message. One way of checking the effectiveness of your system is simply to ask a sample of your callers how comfortable they felt about leaving their messages.

If your answering machine (or phone, for that matter) is used by others (for example, your family), your greeting message, irrespective of whether it is delivered by a person or a machine, should take your business into consideration.

Your income is inextricably linked with your ability to maximise each call of a potential customer. It is therefore proposed that you consider your communication systems seriously in your strategy for growth when developing a business plan. There are other systems currently available that do not attract high costs. These are explored below in detail.

4.6.3 Voice mail

Voice mail is really another version of an answering machine, except that messages are recorded through digital technology rather than using cassette tape-recording facilities. Voice mail facilities are usually available on business telephone systems, as in hotels for example. Other voice mail services are also provided by various mobile phone companies, which divert the callers to your voice mail box if the mobile phone is either engaged, switched off or out of reach.

The more sophisticated telephone systems also have the capacity for the messages to be stored in a voice mail box for different people in the office, who then retrieve their messages via their office phones.

Voice mail facilities enable you to record your personal greeting via your phone and then maintain your messages by either saving or deleting them, also by specially designated codes sent by your phone. As far as the caller is concerned the effect is the same as the popularly known and accepted answering machine technology.

4.6.4 Electronic pagers

Electronic pagers have been around for more than a decade. They have become smaller and are usually placed on a belt or else they tend to get lost. These pagers began to operate mainly in medical and emergency environments by sending just a beep to the holder who was then obliged to phone a central agency or a designated phone number to receive the message. Their sophistication grew in the late 1980s to include alphanumeric characters as part of the message being beamed and received directly by the pager holder.

This is an excellent example of a one-way communication, not unlike writing a letter but far more immediate. At the lowest level of the current technology the caller dials a given phone number, quotes your pager number (usually six digits), and then communicates the message, which the operator immediately beams to you. Your pager beeps continuously, beeps intermittently, flashes and/or vibrates, depending on the type of pager and setting you have selected. It is probably best to train yourself to receive and react with discretion to either beeping or vibrating messages to maximise the value of this technology.

The great advantage of receiving one-way pager messages is that you can respond to the caller at the most convenient time. The downside is the impersonal nature of the caller interacting with an operator and the requirement to quote your pager number.

4.6.5 Personalised pager answering services

There are other versions of the electronic pager technology that have greatly enhanced the initial dialling of your number and the interaction between the caller and the operator.

Rather than having to remember and quote your pager number, it is possible for the caller to simply dial what looks like a normal phone number (but in fact some of its digits are your personal identifiers), and hear this call answered in the name of your practice or your personal name, according to your instructions to the pager service company. Thus, the client's impression is that your assistant or a receptionist answered the call.

At this point of client and telephone operator interaction, the service quality provided by paging companies can make an enormous difference to your business. Some companies take their client satisfaction (that is yourself at the other end now) very seriously and they respond to your needs as a small business operator. They train their staff to answer calls professionally, monitor the number of times a phone has to ring before it is answered, and respond by providing more operators at peak times. Even more importantly, they hold any other information about you and your practice to pass on to your callers as per your instructions. For example, it could include your practice address, what your business does or your fax number. Furthermore, if a client phones and asks a general question without specifically asking to page you, their operator's response will be something like this: 'I am sorry I cannot help you but I can get someone to call you back', and they promptly take the caller's name and phone number, and pass on this information to you via your pager. It is easy to keep a check on them by simply phoning your own pager service and monitoring their operators' responses. There are some who will simply (unfortunately) answer: 'We are only a pager service'. If this service appeals to you, choose the operator company carefully.

While the pager frequency-beaming technologies are very reliable, they are not totally foolproof. Some messages can be missed or get directed to the wrong pager. If, for some reason, your pager was switched off, its battery was low or you might have been in an unreachable spot, it is possible to phone the message recall operator service who will read out the last few messages for you. Beware of putting your pager near a computer or electrical system — your messages may get scrambled. At an extra cost, a printed copy of the last messages, usually limited to a given number of days, can also be obtained. A useful habit to develop is always to check the sequential number of your messages so that if one message is missed you can become immediately aware of this and follow it up with the operator. Another helpful routine that will minimise the potential problems is to replace the battery on a regular basis, for example on the first day of each month, rather than waiting for the 'low battery' signal.

The pager coverage is another factor that you will need to carefully manage and monitor. If you are travelling in country areas, other than the ones designated for your pager service, it is likely that you will miss some messages. It is possible to request that for those limited times the pager coverage gets extended to 'follow you'. Alternatively, if you travel interstate or in country areas on a frequent basis, you may choose instead a larger coverage such as national at the extra cost, which will be more efficient than having to request the extension each time you travel.

The total costs of such a service include the initial investment of around \$300 to \$500 per pager, depending on its type, size and functions. These are usually provided at most competitive prices by companies providing paging services. The basic service where the callers have to quote your pager number is of the order of \$100 per quarter and the additional service of personalised answering by the operator is approximately an additional \$100 per quarter. The prices will vary if you have a number of pagers connected to the personalised answering service and if you request a greater coverage than the one standard area. The total annual cost of having your phone answered professionally and courteously at all times, 24 hours per day, can be as inexpensive as \$800 per year after the initial one-off pager cost.

A personalised pager answering service is, comparatively, a very cost-efficient system, when you consider the costs of purchasing your own telephone system, its normal ongoing costs and the full-time salary.

You may be ready to embrace the idea but do not wish to have this sort of service as your only option. You may wish to answer your own phone when you are available, for example, and use this service when you are otherwise engaged, but you do not wish to advertise many different phone numbers to your clients. Simple solutions to this real dilemma are provided in the discussion of telephone diversions in Section 4.6.7.

The drawback for those professionals whose clients need to make an appointment or change a previously made appointment is that even a personalised pager answering service cannot replace someone who has access to your diary. If your business is predominantly geared to providing one-to-one counselling services, a shared receptionist with a dedicated task of arranging appointments for you would seem a far more effective option than returning all the calls sent to you via the pager. You will also need to consider that you may have to attempt to return some callers' messages a number of times before reaching them.

4.6.6 Mobile phones

Mobile phones have become widely accepted as a norm in our society in relatively few years. They can now fit in your pocket, and the smallest phone in the world at the time of writing is even smaller than a pager. Since their smallness has now superseded the ergonomic necessity of having to hold them in your hand, their size will probably not decrease any further. What will most probably occur, however, is the mobile takeover from other normal phones. Once the networks become more extensive and reliable, there will be one phone for every person rather than one for every home.

The mobile phone has revolutionised the way business is conducted to an even greater extent than the fax did in the 1980s. It has increased customers' expectations of the immediacy of everyone's availability, particularly in the service industry. This has added extra pressures as far as business competitiveness is concerned, and set new standards. Professionals providing psychology or any other services, particularly in the corporate sector, have to be aware of these expectations. As long as your communication systems overall are such that you are able to respond to your clients' calls and satisfactorily deal with their needs, you may never need a mobile phone. There is also an argument that if professionals are too readily available, they send a message to their callers that they do not have much work. There is a need for a subtle balance between satisfying the clients' expectations and not becoming a slave to the mobile phone.

It is not a purpose of this book to explore the etiquette of using mobile phones, but users must be aware of the effect that conducting a conversation on the mobile phone has on those accompanying them. If, for example, you are in a meeting with a client or at lunch with another person, answering your mobile phone tends to send an undesirable message to the person that you are with that he or she is not as important as your caller. You need to resist answering your phone whenever it rings, but this seems to defeat the purpose of having a mobile phone, one may argue. This depends on the purpose for which you choose to use the mobile technology. More specifically, it is your decision whether you control it and use it as a tool to achieve your business strategies or whether it controls your behaviour.

One purpose that a mobile phone fulfils impeccably is to utilise your spare time to return your clients' calls when you would normally not be able to do so. It can also add to the flexibility of your lifestyle without compromising your business. If a mobile phone adds value to your lifestyle by enabling you to play golf or sail more often, then it serves a useful purpose. If it interrupts the few moments you have set aside for relaxation and recovery then it is time to switch it off.

When choosing a mobile phone, it is worth noting that there are two networks currently available in Australia: analog and digital. The phone you select is dedicated to either one or the other. The analog is the older network, which is currently planned to be withdrawn from the market in the year 2000. Understandably, the analog phone is also likely to be cheaper, but the most important considerations in your selection should be network coverage, quality of signal and security. The digital network coverage is increasing all the time but is still behind analog in some country areas. The analog network is more congested, particularly in the city areas and is more easily tapped, as some famous cases have recently demonstrated. Thus, if you plan to use the phone in major cities, the digital network phone is a far better choice, although it still cannot be relied upon to replace your other conventional phone systems.

4.6.7 Telephone diversions

The overall communication system that you will develop to suit your business purposes can utilise the combination of all of the above technology. However, they will only function to their full effectiveness when you link them with appropriate diversion facilities. Telephone diversion technologies enable you to have the best of all options. On the one hand, you can answer the calls personally when you are available; on the other hand, when you are not available the phone may be answered by someone else such as your personalised pager service operator or, at the worst, your voice mail or some other machine.

Furthermore, it is possible to have a number of diversion layers. For example, as the first choice, when you are away from your normal phone the initial diversion can connect the caller to your mobile phone. When your mobile phone is engaged the caller can then be diverted to your pager answering operator. In this way, you can maximise your availability to your clients, especially at the early stage of your business development when you have some spare time to answer your calls. At the same time you eliminate any potential for your clients to find your phone engaged or unanswered.

Proper management of diversion facilities, which are currently available from all telephone companies, is especially vital when your main contact phone is a mobile. This is because current mobile technology means that your phone could be out of range or out of battery charge at least some of the time.

There are four types of phone diversions, all of which fulfil different purposes at various times:

- total diversion of all calls;
- on engaged;
- on unanswered; and
- on out of range or switched off (for mobile phones).

The diversion facilities are obtained by requesting them from the main provider of your telephone systems. They are activated at the telephone exchange, assuming they have such capacity, and so there is no need for substantial investment in special equipment as was the case only a few years ago. The charges for such diversion facilities are made on a call-by-call basis, and they are so minimal that most often they are totally overshadowed by all other phone costs.

Telephone diversion technologies have made it possible to ensure that your business telephone or mobile phone is answered at all times without ever presenting as being engaged to your clients. In addition, it is possible to have quite a complicated system of communication in place, while at the same time presenting only one main phone number to the client.

Permanent diversions are also of great benefit when you move your practice to new premises. For the initial period of time it is useful to activate a total diversion from the old to the new phone number to allow you some time to inform all your clients and change the numbers in all the advertisements and on your stationery. By monitoring the number of diversions actually activated each month on the phone bill, you can phase out this relatively inexpensive facility when it is no longer being used by a significant number of calls. Another service available for such purposes is a permanent recording that identifies your practice and provides the caller with a new number to ring. And an even less expensive and lower level service is a general recorded message that instructs the caller to contact the telephone carrier company to obtain the new number.

4.6.8 Facsimiles

A facsimile machine has become a standard part of the business communication system in the corporate world over the past decade. It fulfils quite a different function from a telephone system and is an additional rather than an alternative consideration.

While a facsimile machine may still be regarded as an optional facility, it is more the norm than the exception. It is not uncommon for virtually anyone, including some individual clients who need to communicate some report to you, to expect that a fax machine is available. Thus the question may be asked: 'What is your fax number?', rather than 'Do you have a fax machine?'. This is especially so since phone/fax machines have become accepted into people's homes.

There are a number of inexpensive alternatives that should be considered as part of your overall communication system. If you have an aversion to 'new' technology and prefer not to invest in a fax machine, you may prefer to set up an arrangement with someone in your local proximity who offers a public fax service. The cost of each fax received will be greater, you will probably be charged per page faxed received, and the extra service may involve being phoned when a fax has been received on your behalf. In this way you can make the fax facility available to your clients without actually owning the machine, but be wary of professional confidentiality under this arrangement. This option, of course, is only feasible if you do not expect many faxes coming in or going out. When you make too many trips to your public fax or get frustrated by its unavailability outside the hours chosen to be open, you will be ready to embrace this technology as one of the inevitabilities of doing business in the twenty-first century.

The next level option is to obtain a combined phone/fax machine. Such a gadget uses one telephone plug and 'intelligently' works out if the incoming call is a fax or a person and answers accordingly. It means that you do not have a separate telephone line dedicated to the fax machine. If you have purchased separate 'boxes', as most people have (a telephone and a fax machine that have not been joined together in the factory), you will need a 'fax switch' to enable the fax machine to switch on if a fax comes in when you are not there to answer it. We advise against this option.

The switch boxes and sharing of phone and fax lines were quite acceptable in the early 1980s when the technology at the time required the person to initiate the call and then press the fax button. Since the current technology expects machines to be talking to each other, a much more efficient method is to connect your fax machine to a dedicated telephone line and relax. This will add to the cost of your practice set-up and so it must be weighed up against the potential.

If you are about to choose a facsimile machine, the main difference between them is the use of plain paper with laser technology and thermal paper. While the thermal paper machine is likely to be cheaper you will need to consider the cost of photocopying each received fax if you need the contents to last for more than a few months. When such paper is exposed to the sunlight, for instance, it tends to fade relatively quickly. Filing them will prolong the thermal fax life a little but you can still expect to look at almost blank pages after a few years.

An alternative to purchasing a dedicated fax machine is a computer fax, which is linked to the modem (discussed further in the following section). The main advantage of a computer fax modem is when the document to be faxed is computer generated. For example, if you have word processed a letter or report and then you need to fax it, you can fax it directly from the computer rather than having to print it and then fax it. In most cases you will probably choose to print it anyway for your file records, which limits the saving potential.

The main limitation of a computer fax is that if you would like to fax anything not generated by a computer, it first needs to be scanned to enable its fax transmission — and for that you need a scanner. Also, unless your computer is switched on, you will not be able to receive the incoming fax.

4.6.9 Electronic mail

Another relatively new area of communication technology that is being embraced increasingly by business and individual users alike is electronic mail, popularly referred to as e-mail. This technology also requires the availability of a computer with a modem. In addition, you will need to subscribe to a provider of Internet type services (for more detailed discussion about the Internet refer to Section 4.12.2). There are an increasing number of service providers who essentially make available to you a space on their computer. The public connection to their computer, which operates 24 hours per day every day, enables it to receive messages and documents others e-mail to you, and the other way around. Others communicate with you by accessing a dedicated e-mail address that uniquely identifies yourself.

The information that belongs to you is stored on the master computer for a limited period of time, and you can access it as often as you wish, to check whether any messages have arrived for you, and whenever you want to send a message to someone else.

The real power in utilising this technology is its speed and the ability to deliver whole documents in a computer format, by 'attaching' them to your e-mail messages, which others can immediately continue editing or print. While this is not likely to excite your individual clients, it is likely to be a real advantage when dealing with corporate clients who can be provided with training materials, assessment reports or other documents you might be asked to prepare via their internal e-mail system networks, which can usually communicate with the public e-mail boxes. Another application of such communication is collaborative project work that you might be undertaking with a consortium of colleagues. Your time can be most efficiently used when you can communicate via e-mail, which enables you to edit parts of various documents without necessarily printing them.

This communication should not be confused with the Internet, which is really a network of computers around the world. Whereas the computers providing e-mail facilities and the Internet may in most cases be the same, e-mail is quite a different channel of two-way communication. If you would like to compare various providers of such services, their prices and modes of operation, magazines such as *Internet Australia*, available in most newsagents, have the entire list of electronic service providers in Australia.

4.7 Initial marketing

Having planned, selected and established a communication system that suits your business and satisfies your clients' needs you will be ready to promote your business. You will now have some assurance that if the promotion works and calls start coming in, your business will have the capacity to respond to those calls and actually provide the services.

This section deals with the initial set-up of the practice involving some basic promotional activities which, presumably, you will have spelt out in the marketing strategy in your business plan. The more elaborate and long-term marketing ideas are presented in Section 6.2.

4.7.1 Promotional brochure

One of the first steps of most practitioners is to produce a brochure whose contents present an outline of the services that the practice provides. While it is possible to develop a successful practice without such a promotional tool, it will certainly help you crystallise in your own mind what your business really sells. It will also be helpful when others to whom you will be promoting your business ask you about what your practice actually does. Before you ask a graphic designer or a desktop publisher to assist you with the generation of your first marketing material you need to be quite certain of what you would like to present in it. In addition to the obvious identification of your practice, with your name, logo, address and contact details, it may include:

- how your services will assist your clients — in what areas, or, in other words, why they should open this brochure and read it;
- what services you provide;
- what other organisations have received your services, if it is directed to organisations;
- who you are and what credibility you have to provide such services;
- how you go about providing your services; and, possibly,
- how much you charge for your services, and method of payment.

There are many different formats of promotional brochures, the most common of which is an A4 sheet printed across the long edge (in a landscape format) and folded in three, making six panels. There are many variations of this basic format, including two A4 sheets (i.e. an A3 sheet folded in half) or a sheet slightly reduced from A4 size. Some graphic designers, printers, desktop publishers and marketing experts will propose more creative designs to ensure that your brochure stands out and is noticed.

Before deciding on the level of design creativity, the purpose for which the brochure will be used should first be identified. For example, are you planning to mail it directly to a number of businesses, individuals, schools or clinics? If so, will you include a letter with it or does the brochure stand on its own? Alternatively, you may always hand deliver the brochure, which will allow you to introduce it to readers and draw their attention to the parts that are more relevant to them.

If you are planning to post the brochure, you will need to invest some effort and creativity in its design to ensure that it receives the attention it deserves. As with your letterheads, the design and content of your brochure will reflect your business and life values. These messages will be decoded by the reader in terms of your commitment to quality, your innovative capacity and the value of your services.

Most readers of marketing material, it seems, are preoccupied with one big question that can be expressed as: 'What's in it for me?'. Your promotional material must somehow answer this question or else it will miss its mark. This realisation that your marketing must be client-need focused can revolutionise your thinking and your design. With this new paradigm you can no longer design brochures talking about yourself but rather about how your services are designed to provide real value to the reader.

If your practice provides a number of different services, some of which may be more suitable to some clients, and you would prefer to build in some flexibility to your promotional brochure, you may consider printing one overall summary brochure with each service outlined on separate pages. This design will enable you to selectively distribute your marketing material in a targeted way to the identified groups of your clients and in this way maximise its impact. If you have a number of sheets each outlining a different service, you may wish to design the summary brochure in such a way that it contains a pocket for the individual sheets.

Be mindful of the ethics of advertising. In particular, see the section of the APS Code of Professional Conduct dealing with advertising. Advertised services should be within your competence, and should not *guarantee* results — particularly if directed to the public. Letter drops are acceptable in the context of 'announcing', and unacceptable in the context of 'advertising'.

4.7.2 Targeted distribution

One of the most fundamental business principles is to inform the marketplace about the products you have for sale. If your brochure serves as a 'product catalogue', you will need to ensure that it gets into the hands of potential clients or referrers of clients. The distribution of your brochures will produce better results for the dollar spent if you carefully target your reader.

In targeting the readership, you select that sector of the market which, in your view or according to your market research results, will have the greatest need for your services. For example, you may distribute to general practitioners in your local geographical area rather than all over metropolitan or country areas as they are more likely to be interested in referring their patients locally. If you are targeting an organisation, you may select the target group by the industry sector, the number of employees, the type of organisation (government, private or community association) or by geographical area.

Depending on your marketing plan, you may commence with a small distribution (100 or fewer) and then conduct an intensive follow-up of all the brochures. Alternatively, you may decide to begin with a distribution of a large number of brochures and selectively follow up those you feel will produce the best results.

In all your direct mail distributions it is quite realistic to estimate your results on the basis of 1% of all the recipients of letters and/or brochures being interested in what you offer, with 0.5% being ready to purchase your product. You can obtain far better results by the careful targeting of your material to those potential clients who have the greatest need or who can readily identify with your practice or your product, but it is quite difficult and costly. It is much cheaper in many instances to distribute larger amounts of the promotional material.

You may well achieve better percentages but it does not pay to expect them. By being more conservative in your estimates you will avoid disappointments and will be able to plan the distribution of your promotional material more effectively. The most common mistake practitioners tend to make is to underestimate the amount of material they need to distribute in order to achieve a reasonable client basis from which to commence a workable practice.

If you are planning a direct mail distribution you need to keep in mind that your material is unsolicited. To increase its chances of being opened and read it needs to somehow stand out from the rest of the advertising material finding its way to each desk every day. You probably receive some unsolicited advertising material at your home. This is because some business marketing expert has identified you as a person in the middle of the target market. When you open the next advertising brochure that appears on your desk you may ask yourself this question: 'What made me open this one and look at it?'. If you have gone further and purchased the advertised product, the next useful question is: 'What was in that brochure that made me want to buy it?'.

4.7.3 Personal follow-up

There is clear evidence that if you include a personalised letter with your promotional literature and if you personally follow up its distribution you greatly increase its chances of success. One of the facts of a people-based business providing intangible products is that the buyer of such a product is unlikely to choose the provider randomly. There are many factors that guide the potential clients' selection processes, but one of the foremost must be confidence in the provider and trust in his or her capability to provide the service promised.

In this light, it is far better to think of all your marketing exercises as relationship building with referrers of your clients or gatekeepers. Such relationship-based marketing takes time to produce results and so you will need some patience, but it is a far surer way to succeed. Such relationships can begin by simply following up the initial letters or brochures you sent. To conduct such a follow-up you begin by simply making a telephone call to the recipient of your marketing letter and requesting a meeting so that you can explain your services more personally. Some persistence will be necessary at times to make the first few appointments. When you get to the next ones you will have some confidence from your past experiences.

It is most important to be prepared for such phone contacts and introductory meetings. By preparing and practising each conversation you will feel far more in charge of the situation. When you do attend an interview with your potential referrer or corporate client, you are likely to leave a more positive impression if you take time to listen to the perspective and particularly the needs of your interviewee, rather than just presenting your services. Once you have commenced a contact with your potential referrers it is important to maintain it so that your presence in the marketplace remains. They may not have had anyone or any project to refer to you at the time you called. Your aim is to have them continue to be aware of your services so that when they do have a need, they can form an immediate association between their need and your practice.

A simple and useful guide for effective communication with potential clients or referrers of clients is contained in *Local Networking and Marketing Kit* published by the APS (1994). This can be purchased by contacting the APS office.

4.7.4 Telephone directory advertising

Yellow Pages or equivalent telephone directory advertising is one of those expenses that you cannot do without, but which is unlikely to prove directly profitable. There are two different sections in most *Yellow Pages* under which you can place your advertisement. The general section simply lists the name of your practice in alphabetical order. The section listing psychologists under the association to which they belong, the main one of which is APS, lists psychologists in the order of their geographical location.

The first general section is a free entry to those who pay for the business telephone line and who nominate their free section as 'Psychologists'.

The other section you need to pay for separately, and you need to contact the relevant association to be included in the listing. The APS listing provides an assurance to the public using the *Yellow Pages* as a guide that the listed psychologists are APS members. While there is no known research about the effectiveness of these advertisements there is anecdotal evidence that being listed under your association tends to produce better results (if any).

Most practitioners tend to agree that advertising in telephone directories does not produce immediate or even long-term visible results. Nevertheless, most practitioners choose to advertise in this way, more for the purpose of establishing credibility. Whereas they accept that clients are unlikely to select them on some random basis from the *Yellow Pages*, it is where they often check if someone has the credentials claimed. If, on the other hand, your practice or name is already known to potential clients they are more likely to choose you rather than use a random selection. Building your public image is therefore important for the long-term success. If potential clients search for a psychologist and have no other means of choosing one, they tend to select on the basis of their geographical proximity. Hence, the suburban guide is also more likely to produce results. Being seen in the *Yellow Pages* or other business telephone directories is one of the first steps in setting up your practice, although by itself this investment may not generate any significant income.

4.7.5 Newspaper advertising

In general, building relationships with the potential referrers of individual clients or projects is by far the most effective marketing exercise. There is a place for advertising in your marketing plan for the purpose of building a name recognition. For example, if you make appointments to see potential referrers as a follow-up of your brochure, they are more likely to agree to see you if they have recognised the name or logo from somewhere else. The recognition factor tends to work even if they cannot exactly recall where they had become aware of your practice.

This phenomenon occurs more powerfully through the television medium although it may not be the most appropriate method of communicating for professional psychology practices.

It does make sense, particularly in the early stages, to place some advertisements, although it is recommended that this is done carefully rather than extravagantly. While signing up long-term ongoing advertisements may be cheaper per placement, it may be difficult to get out of the arrangement when you discover that the desired result has not eventuated. Most practitioners tend to use the local newspaper to build an image in the area from which they practise.

4.7.6 Using local media

In addition to advertising in the local newspaper, you may wish to explore other means of utilising the local media to communicate your message without having to pay for it. The way this works is that local newspapers, like any other media, search for newsworthy items in order to fill their editorial pages. If you are involved in some practice activity such as a seminar, a group or a free talk about a specific subject, this may be newsworthy. To communicate this to the local paper you will need to call the local journalist and discuss it. If you provide a simple summary of what the activity is you will find that by helping the journalist you may increase the chances of publication.

Another way in which you can generate a public image through the local media is by writing articles or letters on a particular subject that may be of general interest. The current interest in issues relating to psychology is increasing rapidly, and most newspapers will co-operate with you as long as you have something of interest to say, and you are not seen to be just promoting your services.

It is important to distinguish between promoting your services and increasing your public recognition in the marketplace. Both activities are important but the latter is an ongoing activity that generates an advantageous environment for the marketing of your services. If you would like to benefit more from dealing with the media, you may find it useful to increase your skills in handling media interviews by attending various seminars that are generally available through the professional development programs or as workshops associated with psychology conferences.

4.8 Registering with insurance systems

4.8.1 Private health insurance funds

If your practice involves provision of counselling or clinical services one of the first activities you must undertake is to register with the relevant health insurance funds in your state or territory. Since Medicare does not refund for psychology services, the only way for your clients to receive any rebates is to use their private health insurance funds. Since you cannot predict which funds your clients have, the best approach is to register with all the funds.

To register with the health insurance funds you need to write to each of them with evidence of your registration to practise. Some funds may have special requirements and application forms to complete. You will receive from them your provider number, which will be different for each fund. This number needs to be quoted on the invoices to your clients. It will also be easier for your clients to receive their rebates if your invoice corresponds exactly to the service item as required by the particular health fund.

Be aware of the rebate levels of each fund as your clients may not be fully informed themselves. If you are a member of the APS, the rates are published from time to time in the the APS Bulletin, and the members of the APS Division of Independently Practising Psychologists (DIPP) are also informed of various changes to fees and rebates through their state newsletters and other communication mechanisms.

The table in the Appendix F presents a sample of current rebates.

4.8.2 Workers' compensation

One of the sources of clientele for psychologists is found in the workers' compensation market. The recipients of compensation through either the state system (in most states known as WorkCover) or the Commonwealth system (Comcare) have access to psychological as well other allied health professional services for which the respective systems pay the practitioner directly.

While some systems pay according to the fees quoted on the invoice, others have their own maximum fee schedules for each professional group including psychologists. Each system has its own unique numbering scheme for each psychology service item. To ensure prompt payment from the compensation system it is important to quote the right service item numbers and charge rates. Some systems may also require that you obtain a provider number as with the health insurance funds. At the time of establishing your practice, it is prudent to contact the relevant workers' compensation authority to be sure of its procedural requirements.

Another way to provide psychological counselling services to workers' compensation recipients is via rehabilitation service providers. Rehabilitation providers can only operate in this field if they are approved by the respective compensation authorities. They provide a wide range of services, which may include psychological counselling. The rehabilitation plan developed by the provider is first approved by the nominated representative of the insurance system. Some providers may have a need to include psychological services on their plans. If they cannot provide such services within their means they may be able to subcontract such services to an independent psychologist. It is worthwhile therefore to establish close working relationships with the rehabilitation providers operating in your area.

4.8.3 Other referring bodies

Crimes compensation tribunals, traffic accident commissions, Department of Social Security (DSS), and the Department of Employment, Education, Training and Youth Affairs (DEETYA) are all useful referral sources. They are often in need of psychological assessments, victim impact statements or assistance for their client group. They are all worth approaching to get the basic information.

Very useful information on the role of psychologists in the Crime Compensation Tribunal and suggested contents of a psychologist's report to the tribunal are contained in the article by MacDonald (1996) — Supervising Magistrate in Victoria.

4.9 Fee schedules

4.9.1 Recognising your own value

Psychologists have traditionally struggled with placing the appropriate price tag on their product (White & Sarfaty, 1970). Historically, most privately practising psychologists had other jobs, some of them full-time (Over et al., 1985). Some provided services from their homes. Partly because of such a historical basis the fees actually charged in the marketplace have varied widely. The part-time practitioners who had other income and who had no administrative overheads associated with running a full-time practice have been able to discount charge rates recommended by the APS.

Another factor resulting in the psychologists' ambivalence in charging high fees has been the recognition that some clients cannot afford professional psychology fees and therefore would have no access to such services. At the same time, some psychology services were being provided free of charge by local community health centres with no means tests.

In such a climate it has been easy to underestimate the value of psychological services, particularly given their intangible nature. On the other hand, the marketing professionals have been sending another message to psychologists. In essence, their message has been: 'People will pay high prices for anything that satisfies their needs, as long as they can perceive its value'. What is the value of better relationships, better health, better performance at work, better functioning teams, the ability to get a job, the ability to think more effectively and therefore lead more effective lives? If you ask your clients to put a price tag on your products, you may be surprised to learn their perception is different from yours.

You, as a service provider need to be comfortable with charging reasonable fees to reward you for the effort you have exerted in providing that service as well as for the time you have spent accumulating knowledge, skills and experience. All of these combine to enable you to provide the sorts of services that your clients need and from which they benefit. In setting your fees you must believe in the worth of your services.

Once you have internalised such value in your own product, the next step of telling clients how much they have to pay will be easy. Marketing experts suggest that you may even help your clients by explicitly pointing out the value of the services they have just received. This can be done perhaps more appropriately by a well-trained receptionist.

4.9.2 Setting your fees

The APS has for some time recommended hourly rates. The current schedule of fees is reprinted in Appendix E.

The calculation of the hourly rate has been based on a number of assumptions. These include that the psychologist operates a full-time practice and incurs all the staff, administrative and premises related costs. When all the expenses and reasonable chargeable time are entered into the equation this rate generates income that is commensurate with a senior clinician's salary. If, however, a particular psychologist does not operate such a practice, it could be argued that the savings in overheads should be passed on to the consumer rather than, as profit, to the practitioner.

As a general rule, the recommended rate should be your guide to setting professional fees. It is quite acceptable and good practice to reflect different types of service and client status in a sliding scale of fees. For example, you may apply different rates to the holder of a health card. The lowest end of your fee could even be free-of-charge work that you perform for charitable organisations, with the limitation placed on the proportion of hours you spend on such work each month.

Some directly paying compensation systems dictate their own rates. From the accounting perspective it is easier to charge the agreed payable fee, although the recommended fee should be shown.

4.10 Collecting revenue

4.10.1 Invoicing clients

Irrespective of what your fee schedule is, it is important to have a clear system for quoting for your services and for invoicing your clients.

An invoice in most cases will be your letterhead (unless you have printed invoice stationery) or at least it should contain all the details that your letterhead does. It is a legal requirement that if you have an ACN number or a registered business name it must appear on the invoice. In addition, invoices should include:

- the name (and possibly address) of the recipient of your services;
- in a compensation case, the client's employer and compensation claim number;
- the type of service provided;
- the date(s) on which the service was provided;
- charge rate;
- your relevant provider and registration numbers; and
- terms of payment (e.g. '7 days nett' or 'Payment in 14 days required').

See Appendix E for more details.

For counselling practices where the client pays, it is best to produce an invoice immediately after the session, for immediate settlement. One of the models that you may imitate is a classical medical practice, where a receptionist completes the service transaction by providing the client with an invoice and a receipt at the same time. A receipt can be in the form of a stamp on the invoice with the words 'PAID', including date, receptionist's signature and the method of settling the invoice.

Some practitioners choose to request payment up front, prior to the counselling session, so that the last transaction with the client is not of a financial nature. This may have some validity if the practitioner is acting as a receptionist as well as a service provider. If you wish to introduce such a system the client needs to be informed and have accepted such a proposition, given that it is unconventional to seek full payment for any item or service prior to its delivery.

In your invoicing system you will need to establish a policy as to when payment is expected. Some clients may expect to take the invoice away and settle it later, some may prefer to pay by cheque rather than cash and others may prefer to use credit cards.

If you would like to provide credit card facilities you will need to contact a relevant bank and/or other credit provider, such as American Express. They will provide you with the vendor's equipment and instructions. You should expect to be charged for each transaction where the credit card facility is used and, in some cases, establishment fees.

For compensation clients your invoices should be forwarded to the relevant authority. You may choose to send your invoices immediately after the services have been provided or to accumulate the charges and bill them on a monthly basis.

Similarly, if your client is a corporate or government organisation, it is reasonable to produce invoices on a monthly basis or as guided by your contract agreement with the organisation. Your services may consist of managing a longer term change management project, employee stress analysis or provision of a series of training seminars. In such an arrangement the payment is usually expected on completion of agreed milestones or the entire project.

When you sign a contract for a longer term project you need to be sure that your finances can withstand the pressure of working for a number of weeks or even months, without receiving any income, while possibly incurring salary and travel costs. There is also a gap between sending your invoice and receiving the payment, which could be a minimum of 14 days and quite possibly 30 days or even longer.

4.10.2 Collecting and managing debt

If you allow clients to pay some time after the invoice has been issued you extend credit to them. In accounting terms they become your debtors. If you have any outstanding debt it must be systematically managed because it affects your business cash flow, which is its blood line.

The first step in debt management is to count the outstanding amount at least once a month. One simple, manual way of achieving this is to keep a sales journal that lists every client and the amount each owes. As each payment is received that amount is deducted from the total amount owed by this client. At the end of each month you can then determine the amount owed by each client.

If you use a computerised accounting system (see Section 4.11), it provides information on your debtors in the following categories defined by the period of outstanding debt: current, 30–60 days, 60–90 days, and 90 days and over. An effective debt management system will ensure that the amounts owed for over 90 days is a very small percentage of the overall debt.

One approach is to issue statements at the end of each month. Statements are very similar to invoices but they include the amounts overdue and the corresponding periods. Some businesses also attach a friendly reminder on the statement, courteously requesting prompt payment. If issuing statements does not bring the desired result, the next step is usually to employ a debt collection agency, who write a stern letter on your behalf requesting immediate payment and reminding your client that prompt payment will prevent further legal costs.

Another approach is to follow up all unpaid accounts by phone, an activity preferably performed by someone other than the professional practitioner. A duplicate invoice or statement can then be issued if the client has lost the original invoice.

If none of the above approaches produces the desired result, you may have to consider writing off the owed amount as a 'bad debt'. If you are reasonably certain that you will not recover some payments, it is best to discuss them with your accountant and act on his or her advice. It is a sobering thought that unless you receive payment for the services that have been charged, it is probable that the business will have to pay tax on this income even though it has not been received.

For psychologists providing individual counselling services, the issue of billing for non-attendance sometimes arises. It is possible to issue an invoice to the client who did not cancel the appointment within the agreed period and has not attended the session. This action is reasonable only if you have clearly informed the client of your policy on payment and non-attendance. It assumes that you have issued the client with a clear statement of your expectations and the rules for cancelling appointments, which the client has read and whose understanding you have checked. Such a statement could form part of your overall policy on payment. Once you have issued an invoice for non-attendance you can pursue its payment in the same way as any other debt.

4.11 Accounting systems

Systematic debt management relies on accounting systems. Irrespective of how large your practice is you will need to consider its accounting needs. In a small practice, it may be possible to keep manual records and present them to an external accountant on a regular basis, for example quarterly. Your accountant, in order to prepare your taxation return documents, will need at least the following:

- bank statements;
- cheque butts;
- bank pay-in books;
- issued invoices and/or sales journal;
- receipt books;
- received bills/invoices from your suppliers; and
- petty cash book.

If you choose to maintain bookkeeping manually, the two most useful records are the cash book and sales journal. These will provide you with a valuable picture of your business performance and are worth maintaining for your information, not just to satisfy your accountant or taxation requirements.

The cash book is divided into two sections, payments and receipts. Each entry corresponds to one transaction of any amount being paid or received. The payment section can be divided into various expenditure categories (or accounts), such as rent, wages and postage. Table 4.1 shows an example of the cash book entry.

Table 4.1 *Cash book: A sample entry*

			PAYMENTS				RECEIPTS			
DATE	DETAILS	CHEQUE/ RECEIPT NO.	Adverti-sing	Insur-ance	Printing	Tele-phone	Wages	Cash	Credit	BANK
										$1000
1 Nov	ABC Printing	001			$150					$850
2 Nov	A. Receptionist	002					$550			$300
3 Nov	Mr Client	999						$100		$400

The sales journal consists of a record of each invoice issued against each client. It can be further split into cash and credit groupings. It is helpful to note that the cash book contains entries relating to actual money received and paid, while the sales journal contains the amounts invoiced. If you do not manage your debt effectively, the sales journal will show large amounts while the cash book will show little cash actually being received. See Table 4.2 for an example of a sales journal format.

Table 4.2 *Sales journal: A sample format*

Date of invoice	Client details	Invoice no.	Invoiced amount		Date paid	Amount paid

If you find the maintenance of such accounting systems time consuming and uninspiring you need to delegate this responsibility to someone with the required vocational interest and skills. You, however, must still be in control of your practice; so it is important to delegate rather than relinquish your responsibility for this important function. One way of ensuring that you stay in touch with the financial performance is to have a monthly briefing with your bookkeeper who may then present you with the key monthly indicators such as:

- income from professional fees;
- total expenditure;
- profit (loss); and
- amount of outstanding debt (e.g. in the category of 60 days plus).

If you would like to see these functions performed efficiently and have the advantage of regular financial reports, you will need to consider computerising your accounting system. The discussion in the following section will provide some insight into the overall computer impact on the professional private practice.

4.12 Information systems

Over the past few decades computers have changed the way business operates. The real information explosion of the late 1980s has made computer technology accessible even to the smallest of businesses. Computers are no longer the domain of the large and most prosperous companies. The word 'computer' has become synonymous with the microcomputer or personal computer, and this is what is meant here by this word (to distinguish it from mainframe computers, usually found in large organisations).

The continuous upgrading of the available technology has produced enormous enhancements in ease of operation, speed and the quality of output. These changes to computer technology, combined with decreasing prices, have meant that the benefits are accessible to those willing to embrace computers for their business or home use.

It is difficult to imagine a professional psychology practice operating efficiently without some assistance from computers. In fact, it will be increasingly more difficult to stay abreast of professional development without some recourse to computer technology, with some conference proceedings, research papers and other up-to-date information being available only via computers.

In your practice, you will either use one yourself or delegate the functions involving computers to someone else. Whichever is your preferred behaviour, it is imperative to be at least aware of how a computer can assist in running your practice. This section is not meant to provide you with a detailed exposé of how computers work, but briefly describe how they can positively impact on your practice.

If you would like to learn further from other psychologists' experience with computers and about their application to private practice, you will benefit from joining a local computer interest group within the psychology profession.

Computer systems, in most general terms, consist of the machinery (the hardware) and the program instructions (the software). Your practice will gain no benefit from the computer hardware unless appropriate software comes with it. To complete the system, you must add people — the programmers and users who need lots of patience and training to achieve what they really want from the computer.

4.12.1 Software

Most popular software is nowadays bundled together with the hardware. This means that you can obtain very cost efficiently most of the generic programs — probably half of your practice software needs — at the time of your initial computer purchase. Other programs can be purchased separately and are available in specialty computer stores, or through various catalogues directly from the distributor. If your identified computer needs cannot be met by generally available software, you may consider contracting a programmer to custom design the solution for your practice. While this will almost always be a more expensive option, its flexibility can outweigh the extra expense.

Whatever way you choose to purchase your software you need to account for its costs in your initial computer budget. When you obtain quotes for computer hardware you should also check the availability and cost of software. As an estimate, it is quite common for all the software to cost as much as the whole computer. Amounts in the order of $5000 should be expected to meet just the software needs for a typical practice. If your needs include computerised testing or powerful statistical analyses, this amount could double. Also, if you plan to operate a number of computers in your practice you need to purchase separate software packages for each, as most of them have a licence to operate on only one computer at any time.

Readers are strongly cautioned against pirated and illegally copied software. It is intellectual property that must be purchased. Its authors deserve their royalty recompense — and you do not want to end up in jail.

The software that is likely to be utilised by professional psychology practices can be divided into ten categories, which are discussed in more detail below.

Word processing

The most basic use of computers utilised by every psychology practice is for word processing the reports, letters, invoices and all other varieties of written communication. The most popular word processing packages appear to be Microsoft Word and WordPerfect. Computers have well and truly taken over this area from typewriters for a number of reasons, the main ones being the flexibility of editing and correcting errors, and the high quality of printing.

If computers are only used for the word processing function they become very expensive typewriters. Such a scenario is somewhat parallel to owning a Porsche only to drive it to a local shop around the corner. The power of today's personal computer is able to deliver far more productivity and efficiency to your practice, if you only care to explore further.

Spreadsheets

A relative newcomer into the English vocabulary is the word 'spreadsheet'. It describes a special kind of software that looks like an electronic page divided into rows and columns. Its main purpose is to perform calculations of a mathematical, financial or statistical nature or any other numerical nature. Essentially it is a very sophisticated calculator, which enables any user to become a programmer. Before the arrival of spreadsheets on personal computers in the mid-1980s all computer programming had to be done using special computer languages. By using simple formulas and English-like expressions it is possible to create spreadsheet-based programs, which can be used as many times as needed to determine some of the most complex or simplest answers to number-based questions.

The most useful applications of spreadsheets in private practice will be in the area of financial and statistical analysis. Its sophistication and ease of use will enable you to apply spreadsheets to, for example, your initial break-even analysis before commencing your practice, and then an ongoing cash flow analysis, which on a monthly basis will determine how much money you need to have in the bank to meet all your expenditure commitments. While it is possible to do this on a calculator, the electronic spreadsheet increases your efficiency in this area, which frees up more time to be spent on productive activities. This method also preserves a record of your basic data as well as your conclusions. The most popular spreadsheets are Microsoft Excel and Lotus 1-2-3.

Databases

'Databases' is also a word introduced by the computer age, and it can be thought of as three-dimensional spreadsheets. Databases are extremely useful tools for holding, organising and reporting information about entities with multiple members such as clients, staff, assets, books and so on. The information relating to such entities is usually made up of many items, referred to as 'fields' such as surname, date of birth, date of first visit, book title and so on. Another analogy that may help in understanding the application of databases is the working of a filing cabinet. Database software provides most efficient solutions for problems that can be painstakingly solved only by filing lots of information in files, which are then grouped into cabinet drawers, which are then grouped into filing cabinets and so on.

The application of database software will depend on your capability to operate it, and your interest in computer solutions. It is, like spreadsheets, another relatively easy to program tool to help you run your business. If you choose to create your own database solutions it will probably be most productive to select one out of many excellent products on the market and become proficient in that one package. Their level of sophistication and power has increased markedly in recent years at the expense of greater complexity and programming difficulty.

Fortunately, at the same time many other databased products have been specifically designed for tasks that previously had to be programmed by the users. One example is a database of clients for marketing purposes. Rather than having to develop a customised solution for your practice, a number of relatively inexpensive software packages are readily available for the task of organising information about clients, for example Tracker.

There are also other database-type products specifically designed for professional private practice, which you will be well advised to consider at the establishment of your practice. Table 4.3 shows a selection of such products currently available. These products contain computerised solutions to managing information about clients, services provided to the clients, and some aspects of financial management such as invoicing and reconciliation of receipts. Some of them have been developed with the specific purpose of servicing a professional psychology practice, while others are more generally applicable to any other practices.

Accounting

While certain office administration packages developed for psychology practices contain some financial management information, none of them can completely replace a professional accounting package. Accounting software is usually general purpose and can be purchased in any software or office stationery store. There are many different packages available and the best approach for selecting one is to base your judgement on its user friendliness, making sure it also provides financial reports that can be effectively used in managing your business.

There have been literally hundreds if not thousands of accounting packages on sale, but recently a handful have become very popular. It would appear that such popularity would not have been possible without some simple design features. Some examples are Mind Your Own Business (MYOB), Quicken, Attaché and Sybiz. You should not find it difficult to locate someone in business who uses one of these packages and learn from his or her experience.

The most common elements found in most accounting packages include:

- Accounts Payable;
- Accounts Receivable;
- General Ledger; and
- Cash Book.

As an addition, extra modules such as Payroll may also be available to add to the system. The greatest benefit from maintaining an in-house

Table 4.3 *Office administration systems (examples)*

Name of package	Name and address of supplier	Contact numbers	Description	Cost	System requirements
Psychologists Administration Management System (PAMS) (Previously PsychMAS)	MasterSoft 1st Floor, 12 River Street, South Yarra, Vic. 3141	Ph: (03) 9820 4467 Fax: (03) 9826 5401	**Complete system:** Reported as being 'a total administrative management system for all psychologists' accounting, case report assessment and administrative needs'. Selection of specific client, therapy and outcome descriptors for statistical overview and report writing. Customised codes (e.g. problem, therapy, testing). Booking facilities, invoice generation, financial record keeping and account management. **Lite version:** Stores client details, invoice generation, financial reporting. An easy-to-use start-up module. **Insurance add-on:** Stores details on insurance claim clients and provides statements for monies owed from insurance organisations. Designed to work in conjunction with the Lite version.	Complete system: $990 Lite version: $390 Insurance add-on: $150	Windows and Macintosh Complete System: Minimum 5 Mb free hard disk space and 6Mb RAM (8Mb recommended) Lite version: 6 Mb RAM (8 Mb recommended) Insurance add-on: Minimum 5 Mb free hard disk space and 4 Mb RAM (6 Mb Minimum 5 Mb recommended)
Medical Electronic Desktop	JAM Software Sydney, NSW	Ph: (02) 9550 0884 Fax: (02) 9564 3353	No information provided by supplier.		
Medidata Version 4 — 1995	Microware 414 Toorak Road, Toorak, Vic. 3142	Ph: (03) 9827 4798 Fax: (03) 9824 1866	Designed to provide patient accounting and practice management for medical profession. Features include itemised accounts and receipts, patient labels/accounting slips, bank deposit slips, doctor's ledger (summary for charges and receipts), monthly statements, letter writer and mailer, practice reporting, listings, waiting room management and patient appointments.	$750. Includes delivery, installation and a manual. Optional training can be provided on site at $45 per hour with $30 per hour travel time. Phone assistance is also available.	DOS or Windows
Quantum Medical System	Waverley Computer Supplies, 311 Stephensons Road, Mt Waverley, Vic. 3149	Ph: (03) 9888 1288 Fax: (03) 9888 1800	A medical accounting system. Features include matching payments, printing of Medicare Bulk-billing Assignment forms and Claim forms, automatic reconciliation of Medicare Bulk-billing payments, automatic calculation of discounts, monthly statements with reminder messages, batch printing of statements per account category (e.g. WorkCover, TAC), unlimited lines of comment for each client.	Single user version: $990 Multi-user network version: $5400 Includes installation and 4 hours of user training. Additional on-site training at $95 per hour plus travelling.	Microsoft Windows compatible. Runs on 286 to Pentium, 640 k RAM, 10 mb disk space

software accounting system is that you can, on a regular and frequent basis, peruse financial reports that provide a snapshot of the health of your business. Such reports will include your profit and loss statement, and balance sheet.

Presentation

A variety of software is available with the specific purpose of generating audio-visual presentation materials. If your practice involves presenting seminars, talks or lectures, the quality of your presentation materials such as slides can be greatly enhanced by such software packages. Such software is also likely to save a considerable amount of preparation time. Some packages now include the complete multimedia functionality, which means that you can embed voice, video clips, and still or moving graphics as part of your presentation. Some of the most popular presentation software include Microsoft Powerpoint (which is included in the Microsoft Office Professional package), Harvard Graphics and CorelDraw.

Once you have generated such images using this software you can either project them directly onto the large screen from your computer or have them printed as overhead slides or 35-millimetre slides.

Graphics

Graphics packages enable you to create some of the most complex images with the greatest of ease and enjoyment. You do need, however, some skills and creativity. Apart from generating your brochures or other material for distribution to your clients it is unlikely that you will use this type of package. As a general rule, since psychologists are not vocationally aligned with artists, this type of activity is better left to more efficient and productive experts.

Desktop publishing

The packages described as desktop publishing are special kinds of software combining word processing and graphics. They provide the user with a tool to generate a more sophisticated layout for documents that have already been word processed and to add graphics, tables or graphs. The best known examples are Pagemaker and Ventura. Unless your practice is involved in the creation of book-quality documents, it is likely that the latest releases of word processing packages will be more than adequate for most of your document work.

Tests

An increasing number of psychological tests have become available in 'soft' computer format in addition to their traditional 'hard' paper-and-pencil types. Even more tests provide the option of computerised scoring. The tests can be administered manually and then either scored at the practice using specially purchased software or sent to the agency providing scoring services. The latter usually takes a little longer but reduces the need for computer investment in-house.

If your psychology practice involves frequent testing, you may consider providing a computer terminal for your clients to access. You will also need to invest in the testing software, which is usually sold on the basis of the number of times it is used, that is per client application (not unlike the paper-and-pencil materials). You can obtain more information from the test distributors. A list of suppliers of psychological tests, with special reference to test software availability, is shown in Table 4.4.

Statistical analysis

Another application of computer software for psychology is statistical analysis. If your psychology product involves designing and administering surveys, you will need an efficient tool for analysing them and presenting reports. If the surveys are of limited quantity and scope, it may be quite sufficient to use the spreadsheet software. Most of the popularly available spreadsheets have built-in sophisticated statistical functions for this purpose. Their capacity for graphical presentation and printing either in combination with word processing software or within spreadsheets is also more than adequate for most of the presentations you will require.

If your practice requirements to conduct survey analysis extend beyond the spreadsheet capacity, you may wish to consider packages that are specifically designed for the purpose of statistical analysis, such as SPSS or Minitab.

Communication

The last category of software applicable to the psychology private practice is generally referred to as 'communication'. This enables computers to connect to each other via telephone cables and modems. For computers to exchange information, a special program is required to control the process of such interchange.

The application for such programs extends to Internet connection, electronic banking, e-mail, computer facsimile or simple data interchange between two computers. Because of the recent explosion of interest in the Internet, most of the communication software that you will probably need is now sold with the computer hardware or by the provider of Internet access services.

4.12.2 Research and communication via the Internet

The word 'Internet' has been propelled out of its past university-based obscurity into prominence in the past few years. Its impact on business, at this stage, is uncertain and has probably been overstated. There is

***Table 4.4** Suppliers of psychological tests*

Name of supplier	Address	Contact numbers	Description of available software	Cost of software
Australian Council for Educational Research (ACER)	19 Prospect Hill Rd Camberwell, Vic. 3124	Ph: (03) 9277 5656 Fax: (03) 9277 5678	Specific test packages, e.g. MBTI, SDS	
Psychological Assessments Australia (PAA)	Suite 3, 15–17 Forest Rd Hurstville, NSW 2220	Ph: (02) 9589 0310 Fax: (02) 9589 1062	Microtest Q Assessment System: Scores, reports results and stores information for 14 different assessment instruments (e.g. MMPI, QOLI, MCMI-II, CISS). Client does test directly on computer, psychologist enters score by hand or scans the results in with a scanner. Scoring/reporting is charged on a per use basis (report counter attached to printer).	$200 annual licence fee. Upgrades are free.
The Psychological Corporation — Harcourt, Brace & Company	30–52 Smidmore Street Marrickville, NSW 2204	Ph: (02) 9517 8999 or 1800 263 951 Fax: (02) 9517 2249	PsyTest Assessment Management System: Administration, scoring and reporting of Beck scales, Millon Index of Personality Styles and MicroCog: Assessment of Cognitive Functioning. Client does test directly on computer or psychologist enters score by hand or scans the results in with a scanner. Scoring/reporting is charged on a per use basis (report counter attached to printer).	$450.95 for complete kit, includes User's Guide, Quick Reference Card, Software Update/Warranty Registration Card, Diskettes and Use Counter.
Saville & Holdsworth Pty Ltd	37 Alexandra Street Hunters Hill, NSW 2110	Phone numbers: NSW (02) 9816 2233 Vic.: (03) 9820 1788 Qld: (07) 3369 8832 SA: (08) 331 8011 WA: (09) 375 2567	Most psychological tests available on computer. Tests that are not presently available on computer will be available in this form in the next 12 to 18 months.	Varies depending on test.
Science Research Associates Pty Ltd (SRA) SRA McGraw Hill Book Company P/L	4 Barcoo Street Roseville, NSW 2069	Ph: (02) 9417 4288 Fax: (02) 9417 7003	Contact SRA for specific tests available on computer.	

little doubt that the impact of electronic communication will continue to increase in almost every area of our lives, business included. Rather than explaining the Internet, which has been the subject of many informative books (e.g. Kent, 1994), its application to psychology practice will be discussed here in two main areas: research and communication.

The Internet is essentially a collection of computer networks around the world. It is maintained by an array of satellite links, computer cables and numerous telephone connections. Through this network it is possible to gain access to a number of databases containing valuable research information and communicate with millions of other individuals of like interest.

To gain access to the Internet you need to contact one of the many providers, and it pays to compare their prices. They will usually provide you with all the software you need to communicate with their central computer. You will also need a modem connected to your computer. The retailers of modems often include a free trial period of connection to a particular Internet provider, which is a very cost-efficient way to try it and see if it has some appeal to you. Apart from the one-off account establishment fee, most of the providers charge for the connection on an hourly basis.

At the lowest level, communication can take place by a simple e-mail connection, which your Internet service provider will make available as part of the normal access for a small fee. Using e-mail is equivalent to electronic faxing or writing to someone — you need to know who the addressee is. It is simply another written form of communication but it is extremely fast and inexpensive. Because the connection to your provider's computer is usually local if you are located in a metropolitan area, it means that an international e-mail costs you no more than a local call and a few minutes connection to the computer.

Another type of electronic communication is newsgroups and bulletin boards. These provide an opportunity to relate to people of similar interest and exchange views on various subjects with vast numbers of people at the same time. There are many such newsgroups designed by and for psychologists working in specific professional areas around the world.

One of the most popular parts of the Internet is the World Wide Web. This is a network of computer sites containing all kinds of documents consisting of text and/or images. Through your Internet access program, referred to as a browser, you can find numerous documents that other people have placed for you to read. Anyone can place information on his or her computer, which is referred to as 'home page'. This forms a site that anyone else in the world can 'visit' or 'browse'. There are many web sites of interest to psychologists, which provide further opportunity for useful information exchange. A list of some useful sites related to psychology can be found in Appendix C.

Two cautions need to be made. One is that there is no guarantee of the provenance and integrity of Internet information; the second is to be alert to giving private information and contracting electronic viruses.

As an Internet user, you will be able to establish your own 'home page' on which you can publish your articles or inform anyone about any subject you might be interested in. This is the area of interest to most businesses, which can see it as an opportunity to advertise and market their products. For psychologists, the whole Internet experience can provide a great opportunity to network with others and exchange ideas, thus reducing the feeling of isolation in private practice. At the same time it can provide an extremely efficient tool for researching a particular topic of professional interest and keeping oneself abreast of the latest information in the world without spending any time away from the practice.

Information placed on the Internet by universities and other organisations may provide a reasonable starting point for researching a particular topic of interest. You can also perform comprehensive literature searches via computer-linked library resources for which there are extra charges. In this case you use the Internet as a gateway into the desired library abstract resources.

4.12.3 Hardware: Choosing the right computer solution

The choice of a computer system is often shrouded in mystery although it is no different from purchasing any other piece of machinery, which has to provide for the user what is expected from it at an optimum cost. One of the mistakes you can make is to select one on price alone. You would not do this with a car, for example, or any other large purchase. Before you start comparing the prices you should determine your needs and identify the criteria on the basis of which you will make your selection.

The first question that any computer salesperson will ask is 'What will you use it for?'. If you are unsure, look through the ten categories of computer software, discussed in Section 4.12.1. You will then need to determine what proportion of time your computer will be used for in each of those areas of activity. For example, if your computer is mostly going to be used for word processing and very little for accounting and testing, you will not need the speed normally required for fast calculations in financial and statistical analyses. In other words, your needs for software will define your hardware needs. There is no point purchasing a computer that does not perform well for the software you need.

Software actually drives your hardware needs. You must be aware that programs continue to evolve, and with their constant enhancement they require more from hardware: more memory, more disk space or faster processing speed. Keeping this in mind, it may be a costly error to purchase a superseded computer model merely because of the attractiveness of its price. While this may be a reasonable decision when purchasing a car, as it is still likely to meet your expectations for driving you around in many years' time, it may not be the case with your computer. Unfortunately, their depreciation is so steep that in two or three years your computer may be difficult to give away, not to mention selling.

One of the first choices you will need to make is between Macintosh or IBM-compatible technology. There is less and less difference between the two technologies as far as the user is concerned. While some time ago Macintosh machines were far easier to use and were particularly good at graphics work, the field has now equalised with IBM-compatible machines becoming faster and providing an easy and consistent Microsoft Windows interface. In general, the business world has embraced IBM technology, with the exception of creative industries such as advertising. Schools have been the predominant users of Apple and later Macintosh technology. Most recently many schools have commenced introducing IBM-compatible technology to prepare their students better for their entry into jobs in the corporate sector. Depending on which area of practice you specialise in, it may be an important factor for your computer systems to be compatible with your corporate clients.

One of the barriers to overcome in purchasing computer hardware is the jargon that salespeople tend to use, as it were, to extend their control over unsuspecting newcomers into the field. It pays therefore to do some research before committing yourself to a particular purchase. There are a few basic facts about computer hardware that may be of some assistance when making your selection. The computer systems are made of the following components:

- *The central processing unit* (CPU) is the heart of any computer. Its size is expressed in 'bits', which represent the way the computer handles information for its processing. Currently 32-bit machines are on the market, and there is little point in purchasing any less powerful ones. The size of the CPU is also expressed as 286, 386, 486 and Pentium (in IBM-compatible machines). For business purposes any CPU less powerful than a Pentium will be out of date too quickly to contemplate purchasing it. All CPUs have clocks that dictate the speed for their information processing, and clock speed is measured in megahertz (MHz). The faster the CPU speed the faster the computer will operate, and so, in general, it is safest to select the largest and the fastest CPU currently available on the market. It is likely to be superseded within a few months of your purchase, which will mean that the software developers will also release an enhanced version of the software, which will demand more disk space and memory, and so the cycle continues.

- *Random access memory* (RAM) is the place where most of the information processing takes place when computers are in operation. It is a temporary area and its size determines the amount of information that can be worked on at any one time. RAM is measured in megabytes (MB), and one megabyte can store one million bytes or characters. The more memory the better, because it will allow your software to run faster, and some popular programs described above now recommend at least 16 MB RAM to run efficiently. Purchasing a computer with more RAM than the standard offer will generally assure your system of better performance and longer durability. You will need at least 16 MB RAM to run multimedia effectively.
- *Hard disk* storage is the device in which the information is stored permanently and from which all programs are imported into RAM when you switch on the computer. As the software becomes more sophisticated, it also becomes more voluminous, and so there is likely to be a growing need for larger disk sizes. The new standard is likely to be more than 1 gigabyte (1000 MB) and if you must settle for any less it should not be much less.
- *Floppy disk drives* are flexible storage devices, which currently are 3.5 inches (8.9 centimetres) in size and 1.44 MB in storage capacity. One such drive is required as a minimum to be able to copy programs onto the hard disk and provide back-up facility.
- *CD-ROMs* are compact disks with read only memory information. They have a greater capacity for storage than floppy disks. CD-ROM technology is increasingly used to hold large amounts of data such as telephone books, collections of research documents, and the Australian Bureau of Statistics Census information. Software is also distributed using this medium rather than multiple floppy disks. CD-ROM drives are usually sold in conjunction with multimedia kits including stereo sound cards and speakers. Given that CD-ROMs have become a standard item in a computer system it is more often utilised by various software packages.
- *Monitors* display information to the user. They are also referred to as visual display units (VDUs) or just screens. The two main considerations with VDU purchase are resolution and colour. Resolution represents the number of pixels (dots) that make up the image on the screen — the higher the resolution, the clearer the image. The resolution is expressed as the number of horizontal pixels times the number of vertical pixels (e.g. 800 × 600). Colour monitors also have ranges of colours available and the higher resolution monitors have more colours. Most high-quality software demands a range of colours.
- *Printers* are vital machines that will determine the quality of all your output produced by your computer. Currently the three most popular types of printer available on the market are dot matrix, ink

jet and laser. Laser printers provide the highest quality and the most consistent output. Their performance is compared mainly by speed, measured in pages per minute (e.g. 8 PPM), and dot resolution, measured in dots per inch (e.g. 600 DPI). Ink jet printers spray ink onto the paper through nozzles to produce dots forming the characters, and their speed is measured in characters per second. Dot matrix printers are of the lowest quality and should be considered only for draft or internal document printing such as accounting reports. It is recommended that laser printers be considered as a standard for any business purporting to provide quality professional services. Colour printers are also available; however, the cost of high-quality laser colour printers is still prohibitive although it is likely that they will become standard in the foreseeable future. The currently available colour ink jet printers provide reasonable colour quality, but they tend to create a compromise in normal black printing quality and printing speed. Colour also increases the cost of the printing of each page.

When you have chosen the computer package that you believe will meet your need it is time to consider post-purchase support and warranty offered by the retailer. It is often more valuable than the short-term saving on the total price. The hardware cost for one computer is likely to be of the order of $5000.

Remember, when negotiating, that add-ons are cheaper. Buying your software and hardware from the same place is an excellent opportunity to get substantial discounts. If you get a package deal, *do* get the original floppy disk of your software *and* the manuals. They not only are valuable but also are an indication of genuine ownership.

4.12.4 Computer administration

You need to undertake some essential tasks to ensure that your computer investment serves you well. Computers are just machines, and as such they are fallible. Disks crash, files get corrupted and even viruses get transmitted. It is best to avoid problems by conducting regular back-ups and checks of your system.

Backing up your computer hard disk is probably one of the most important functions that will prevent small problems becoming potential business disasters. There are some simple rules to follow when creating a back-up of your work:

- Always keep at least two back-up copies, usually the latest and second latest versions — in this way, if a crash occurs during your backing up you will still have one good copy.

- Always back up your data (documents, accounts, test results and so on). They are most vulnerable because they will be either irreplaceable or very costly to reproduce. The purchased software can always be reloaded from the original diskettes (or their copies).
- Always keep at least one back-up disk (or tape) off the premises where the computer system exists. Storing a back-up with the computer is as good as not having a back-up at all in cases of burglary or fire. To sharpen your thinking and commitment to keeping effective back-up, imagine that the next day when you come into your practice, the computer is gone — and then ask yourself how quickly can you restore the entire system on a new machine.

It is also prudent to check your system regularly for viruses and other possible problems, and always check other people's floppy disks before loading them onto your system. There are a number of effective virus-checking software packages available. One way to ensure that these computer administration tasks are done is to delegate it to an expert who spends a few hours every month to keep your system in perfect health. The back-up must be done on a daily basis.

5 Developing practice excellence

All businesses go through a life cycle of identifiable phases: infancy, growth, getting organised, maturity, decline and cessation (Stanley, 1993). Each phase can last for a variable period of time, and it is not easy to predict its duration. It is useful to recognise the phase that your practice is in, and behave accordingly, to assure it of corporate longevity.

If you have already established your practice following the principles outlined in Chapter 4 you have entered the initial stage, 'infancy'. This phase is likely to be quite exciting and demanding of your time and energy. In the business infancy stage you will probably be willing to invest both time and energy, in the hope that your life will in fact be better for it. As time goes on, you will inevitably discover that the demands the practice places on your time continue to increase, and that you cannot easily control the growth of your practice. The frustrating part of it all will be that, despite you working harder than ever before, you are actually making less money. The whole experience of gaining income from your practice may become very uncertain and unpredictable.

When you reach the point of feeling tired of trying to make it succeed, and the need for a holiday from it all becomes an obsessive thought, it is time to stand back and take a serious look at the way in which you run your practice. If you have never reached this point it may be because you have been able to take serious looks at your business regularly throughout its development. At those times you might have discovered that the only way to retain your sanity and enjoy the challenge of generating your own income from your efforts is to start thinking of your practice as a system.

5.1 Developing business systems

In his very readable management book, Michael Gerber (1995) proposed a new paradigm to enable a business to produce the desired outcomes for your life. His proposition is to think of the business itself as a product, so that it can be franchised. The franchise model means that your practice could be conducted by anyone else who chose to purchase it from you.

There are possibly some limitations to this paradigm in its application to professional practices, which have intense person-to-person interaction inbuilt. If your business is totally dependent on you and cannot function without you, then it really is no business at all. It has become your life and it will probably control your life rather than you using it to achieve your life's principal goals.

If your business is to function independently of you as a system it needs to have predictable components and it needs to deliver consistently high-quality product to its customers. Applying the franchise paradigm to your thinking about your practice will lead you to design it in such a way that your clients will be able to expect and receive service of the same quality every time. When they tell others about you, that same expectation about what and how you deliver your services will be met.

This transition of your practice into a predictable system of service delivery can be thought of as a phase of 'getting organised'. While you may be providing quality services to your customers at the moment, check if it is happening by accident or by design. Let us explore some questions to help you define the extent to which your practice is organised as a system:

- Do all your clients hear the same greeting when they phone you?
- If you are not available, are all clients given clear alternatives as to how to establish contact with you?
- Are all your clients given the same and clear explanation as to what to expect during the sessions?
- Are all your clients greeted when they come to see you and looked after in the same way every time?
- Are all your clients able to make appointments with you when they need to, and are they all provided with a card identifying the date and time of their next appointment?
- Are all your clients billed for the services in the same way, given invoices and receipts of the consistent format, and offered the same payment options?
- Are all your suppliers' bills paid within their specified credit terms?
- Do all your staff know what your expectations are of their performance?
- Do all your staff receive their pay at the same time and on a regular basis?
- Is the same level of courtesy extended to all of your stakeholders?
- Are correspondence and requests dealt with promptly?

The overriding question here is whether your clients can have the assurance that they will receive the same level of service every time they make a contact with your practice. In stepping back and taking a look at your business, you need to look at it from your client's point of view.

5.2 Customer focus

To be able to appraise your practice from your clients' perspective, you need to first identify who your clients are. Because of the nature of psychology business, in addition to the primary individual clients quite often there are secondary clients or client organisations/systems that actually pay for your services. Examples of such scenarios are compensation systems or employers who pay for your services delivered to their claimants and employees, respectively. See, in particular, *The Professional Psychology Handbook* (Francis & Cameron 1996, Chapter 9). It is worthwhile re-emphasising here that an identification of *who is your client* is crucial.

A parallel scenario for an organisational psychologist is where the Human Resource Department is funding a project involving numerous other clients — managers and supervisors, and team members of work groups, and such like. Your services to each of these groups of clients are important although only one of them will transact the payment for your business. Other hidden clients in an organisational setting are also the superiors of those who have contracted your services, such as the Board of Directors, although you may never meet them face to face.

There are also other individuals or groups who are decision makers regarding the referral of the individual clients to your practice. They form your indirect clients who also, nevertheless, need to be considered when you become customer focused. At this point of your business, 'becoming organised', you need to identify the expectations of all types of your clients and ensure that the way your business meets their expectations is professional and consistent.

This assumes that your value system contains a certain commitment to excellence in all your endeavours, but particularly in relation to your clients' expectations. You may have had experiences where you as a customer were impressed by the level of commitment given to quality or when the opposite happened. It will be worthwhile to analyse each of those experiences in every shop, hotel or solicitor's office you have visited. How did you feel as a customer? What specific experiences made you feel like returning to the same service provider? Were your expectations met? Were you aware of any expectations you had prior to your contact with the service providers?

You will probably discover that the process of satisfying customers is mostly unconscious. The transactions that take place between the provider and the receiver are nevertheless quite powerful. How clients feel about the service they receive is far more important than what they process at the cognitive level. Their feelings about the whole transaction are often determined by the smallest detail, which you may completely miss, unless you begin looking at your business through your customers' glasses.

In a psychology practice all your clients — direct and indirect, primary, secondary and tertiary — must be considered as your customers. Each one of them has a potential to help your business succeed by referring others, returning for more of your services or contracting your services in a project.

5.2.1 Charting the customer-service process

Clients come in contact with you and your practice in many different ways. Your behaviour towards them will form a lasting impression that will impact on your business. To ensure that all points of contact with clients promote a positive image that encourages them to continue the client–provider relationship, they have first to be identified.

One way to begin is to draw a line representing the clients' journey along which they pass a number of points of contact with your practice, starting with the initial phone call, arriving at your premises, finding a place to park the car, entering through the door, and so on. At each point they experience feelings relating to their interaction with your practice. Follow this journey with them, through their eyes and list all sorts of little details that will potentially make big impacts on their experience.

At each point of contact, there are events that can be controlled by your business system. How clients are greeted, what options are given to them at the reception and how their questions are answered are all examples of such events that can be identified and presented as a chart of activities. Such a chart will show who is responsible for which activity and how one activity is connected with another. Some of them will show a number of options leading to a few activities, depending on the preceding scenarios.

The customer-service process chart will be easily recognised by the organisational practitioners who assist their client organisations to achieve better performance and continuous improvement in their processes. There is no reason that the same change intervention tool could not be applied to a much smaller organisation — your practice. The teaching of applied psychology provides a solid basis upon which to create practice systems that aim for excellence. Such generic but dormant skills are available for the process of running a business. Your underlying technical knowledge of human behaviour, and its biological basis, can be put to good use in becoming a change agent within your own practice.

5.2.2 Initial contact

One of the small but vital details that can often make a big impact on the client's perception of quality of service is the experience of the first contact. This may take place through a phone call, a personal visit or even a written request. How your practice is presented in that initial contact will remain in a client's perception with the power of a classical primacy effect.

To maximise the positive impact on the client, you need to develop a system for responding to new contacts. First, you will need to define the perception that you would like the new or potential client to form about your practice. For example, the condensed message you might like to communicate could be: *We are caring, we are professional, we offer quality*. Whatever the message, you can develop systems to ensure that at each point of contact with a client this communication takes place effectively.

It cannot be overemphasised that a discreet manner is vital in psychology. Talking loudly at reception, for example, can be acutely embarrassing to clients. The information they volunteer and the questions you pose should be inaudible to others.

In developing a system that will deliver your message there is a need for innovation, documentation, implementation, training and monitoring. The results of monitoring will lead to further innovation, and so on. The system of delivering excellent service is a continuous process that must evolve to meet the changing needs of your clients. If, instead, the process of initial contacts with your clients is not systematised, it is left to chance.

Your receptionist staff, your network, books and articles will all play a part in creating an innovative way to greet a client, to ask the right question. For example, a greeting beginning with the words: 'How can we help you?' may lead to better results than simply 'Good morning'. When a client asks for an appointment with Psychologist X, the response may be: 'Have you seen Mr/Ms X before?', which may then lead to another selective response or the providing of a handout, depending on the answer to the initial question.

The system exists only if it can be replicated with reasonable predictability, and this can take place only if the agreed innovation is documented in some form. It can be an instruction sheet to the receptionist, for example. Such an instrument can be used in a short training session and displayed in a prominent place in the office. If the system works well, and your regular receptionist is replaced by a temporary assistant, that person will be able to follow the instructions quite easily. In a business system, there should be few surprises and few assumptions. If anything is left to chance, you will not be able to predict, and to assure your clients of a consistently high-quality experience.

The monitoring of a system of initial contact will involve some behavioural observation, measurement and analysis. You cannot assume that the operational procedures are followed simply because they are written down. The overall practice system needs to include some counting and measuring. This is another area where a universal psychology training in statistical and scientific methods of measurement should provide a valuable advantage for a psychologist in business.

Your measurement of compliance with the procedures may include ongoing collection of data, regular surveys, random checks, or a combination of these and any other creative methodology. Their aim is to ensure that the written procedures are followed, as well as to provide some basis for evaluating the extent to which your innovations with client contact have been successful. By consistently collecting relevant data over a period of time, and experimenting with different greetings for example, you will be able to determine trends that will tell you how effective your innovations are. Then you can establish systems that really work for you, not by guessing but by testing the system and adjusting it.

5.2.3 Information on entry

Another milestone in the life of the client–provider relationship is the moment of the first appointment during which some transaction takes place and service is provided. It is a significant moment of truth. For many clients, it may be the very first time they have consulted a psychologist, and their experience may be loaded with uncertainty and anxiety. The information the client is given at the point of entry into your practice may reduce or heighten this state.

By applying a systematic innovation approach you could determine the types of questions most clients wish they could have asked at the first interview, but were afraid to. You may obtain a list by simply talking to your clients or talking to other psychologists and combining their intuitive knowledge. Your system solution could be a reader friendly handout, which would be given to clients on their first visit.

The issues covered by such a handout may include:

- What is involved in a consulting session?
- How long will each session be?
- How many sessions will I need?
- How much will it cost me?
- How and when do I pay?
- Should I (or could I) bring my partner and/or my children?
- Will you use some personality tests?
- What will be expected from me during the consulting process?
- Will I be given any homework?

- Will I be given any written reports about me?
- Will our discussion be confidential?
- Will you record our session on a tape recorder?
- What happens if I cannot come to my next appointment?

The handout addressing the above issues could be read by clients while waiting for their first session. There may be many other ways of reducing clients' initial anxiety and of providing useful information to them at the same time. The approach suggested here is simply an example of applying innovation and systems to ensure that each client has a high-quality, positive experience with predictable consistency. The process of continuous innovation and its systematic application will lead to excellence in practice.

The Professional Psychology Handbook contains a 'Statement of client rights'. You may choose to use that statement or have it on display. Such an explicit expression of caring can only be beneficial.

The information transaction at the point of entry is two way. Your system will probably require certain information about the clients regarding their demographics, source of referral and compensation status. The first-time client will need to complete a form, probably designed exclusively for your practice. You may wish to determine the most acceptable means by which this information can be obtained, while at the same time sending the desired message to the client about your practice. For example, should it be a self-administered form or should a receptionist ask the questions and interact personally with the client at the same time? Unless you ask your receptionist and your clients some questions about how the process works now, you may never know how to improve it.

For an organisational psychologist, the entry to an organisation may mean something quite different from a client entering a counselling/clinical practice. The relationship with the client organisation may start with a visit to the organisation's premises. The initial phase of the consulting process will be referred to as 'entry'. The principles of a service system apply to this scenario perhaps even more powerfully. Your behaviour at every step will demonstrate your practice's commitment to excellence. The consistency of this behaviour is just as important in shaping the clients' perception of you as a service provider and influencing their experiences. By providing a brief summary about your approach to consulting, a simple statement about your philosophy and how things are done at your practice, you will create an opportunity to check the clients' expectations. You can further check your understanding of their expectations and project objectives in a written confirmation — each time new objectives are discussed. Most importantly, if you have set your clients' expectations you must have a system that can assure you of their fulfilment.

Systems for effective consulting in organisations that can be easily adapted to any practice may be found in a number of useful texts, for example Block (1981).

5.2.4 Receiving payments

The process of receiving payments from clients is another step of the service provided by your practice that lends itself to a systematic approach. Any ambiguity and embarrassment involved in the financial transaction of payment for services rendered needs to be eliminated from the process.

The first step towards this objective is to clearly explain the options at the initial contact or the first session, verbally or through a handout. Following a session the client needs to know if the payment is now expected and, if so, how this is to be done. Some of the questions that may be in the client's mind at this point are:

- Must I pay now or can I pay later?
- Do I get a discount if I pay now?
- Can I pay by cheque?
- Can I pay by credit card?
- Who will receive my payment?
- Will I get a receipt?
- Can I get a refund from Medicare or my health insurance?
- Will my compensation claim cover the payment?

Your system of practice excellence will ensure that each client will be informed about the process of payment, and that each client's question will be answered courteously by a trained receptionist. The payment system will need to ensure that the receptionist is aware of the client's name, compensation status and other payment-related data at the time of leaving the consulting room. This will reduce the client's waiting time, and will also instruct the receptionist about how to deal with a number of simultaneous demands: the client waiting to pay while there are new clients being served at the counter (who will presumably take longer to process), and the ringing telephone. This scenario may prove to be a useful and immediate test of the level of your practice's capability to deliver quality service with consistent predictability. Which of the following would your receptionist do if faced with such conflicting demands?

- Interrupt the new client and ask that he or she waits while the paying client is served.
- Acknowledge the paying client and ask that client to wait while continuing to serve the new client.
- Ignore the phone and finish serving the new client.

- Answer the phone and ask the caller to wait, and then finish serving the new client.
- Politely interrupt the new client, answer the phone and then process the paying client before returning to the new client.

There are many possible permutations and many opportunities for the receptionist's own initiative and decisions. Out of all the possibilities there are only a few that will communicate the desired message about your practice. Since it is your practice, you need to design a system that will make sure your message gets out. The only sure way to do this is not to leave the receptionist's behaviour to chance.

One hears a universal criticism of staff who give primacy to telephone calls when someone is waiting for personal attention. This is doubly annoying when the phone interrupts a face-to-face conversation and the staff member ranks the person present as second.

In a situation where you play the role of a receptionist, after hours or when your receptionist is not available, the same applies to you. It is possible that you do not know the office systems and communicate the message: 'We practise in chaos'. If you perform the role of a receptionist, it is up to you to follow the procedures.

In an organisational psychology practice setting, the same principles apply, with the difference being the lack of personal contact at the reception counter. The communication about your practice nevertheless happens when you issue invoices: their appearance; their content; the amount of detail about the service you have provided; the frequency of invoices being issued; the client's met expectation about the total amount; and the milestones achieved prior to billing. All of these add up to the client's approval of, or disappointment with, the payment process.

5.2.5 Making new appointments

Making new appointments for clients is another important activity in your practice — client interaction. The first aim of a systemic approach is to ensure that the client has no doubt about the date and time for which the appointment was made. The second aim is to make sure that the practitioner has the time written in a diary, so that there is no possibility of the appointment being double booked or the practitioner not being available.

Your approach to making appointments should at least address the following questions:

- Is it a practitioner's or a receptionist's role to make appointments?
- Is it a combined role, with the practitioner establishing the general period following which the booking should be made, and with the

receptionist actually identifying the specific time slot and writing it in the appointment book?
- Whose role is it to write on the business card the date and time of the next appointment?
- Is the client informed about the cancellation rule, the consequences of not turning up for an appointment without giving notice, and the acceptable length of time for cancelling before the appointment to avoid any penalties?
- Is a map identifying the practice address and parking forwarded to the first-time client?
- What are the rules about appointments after hours?
- Does the receptionist have a complete basis upon which to make appointments without referring to the practitioner?

There are probably some other questions that you and your staff can raise when you focus on this part of the practice system. Once they become known in the collective minds of those who determine the level of service delivered to your clients, they need to be systematically answered, documented and then enacted.

5.2.6 Practice environment

The physical environment of your practice will very powerfully and immediately send a message about your practice, before the client even walks in. Its outside appearance, the signage, the lighting, paint colour, the carpet and all the physical characteristics combined provide the client with information about your practice.

The reception area needs to engage the client immediately upon entry with appropriately placed signs and a greeting. Any ambiguity about what is expected of the client upon entry should be meticulously eliminated. The directions to the waiting area, the reception, toilets, public telephones and so on need to be clearly marked.

Further attention should be given to engaging the client in interesting activity while waiting. This can be done most easily with up-to-date magazines and/or reference books on special-interest topics placed on a coffee table. A television set may also be an effective way to ensure that your clients are engaged while waiting. A carefully selected and educational video can be played instead of the television programs.

Special attention must be paid to public safety and cleanliness. A close observance of the practice's orderly and clean appearance is not costly, but it does require an attitude and commitment. There is a need to clearly identify those responsible for the pleasant appearance of the waiting room, and an orderly arrangement on the magazine table and, particularly, children's toys. The cleaner's performance also needs to be monitored and fed back to encourage attention to detail.

Since your business deals with human factors of all kinds, it may be of interest to obtain some research on the effect of the physical environment on your client. This sort of research is, after all, in the psychology domain, and so part of your innovation process could be based on some well-documented scientific evidence.

5.3 Quality systems

To take your practice business system to another level, you may consider what it would take to obtain quality accreditation under the International Standards Organisation — ISO9000 — for your practice, although those processes are primarily designed for large organisations. Irrespective of whether or not you actually undertake the task, merely thinking about it may shape the way you do things in your practice. This sort of thinking is quality thinking. There are a number of quality management books, taking a very practical approach to quality systems (e.g. Kruithof, 1993; Kruithof & Ryall, 1994).

The process charting described in Section 5.2 in reference to customer service should be applied to all other processes in the business, including administration, marketing, training and development, people management, and performance review. The process chart will form the foundation of the operations manual for your practice. Each activity in the chart will be described in specific behavioural terms, so that the person responsible for each activity will have a clear understanding of your expectations.

The operations manual will form the basis of induction and ongoing skills training for each staff member. Too many business operators rely on ad hoc verbal instructions, often communicated in a hurry in between appointments and other urgent tasks. Training of staff, particularly at the induction stage, is critical to the business function. It falls into the *important but not urgent* category of tasks. Staff training is so much more effective when it is structured and built into your elementary business systems. This is achieved by linking the training to the practice operations manual. There is no better way to do this.

The operations manual can also define measures of each significant task. The measures are designed to clearly indicate the extent of compliance with the procedures and the level of work quality. These performance indicators must be easily obtainable and few in number, and as specific and concrete as possible. If they are designed with clarity and communicated explicitly, they can be used for regular staff reviews with great effectiveness. Used in this way, the operations manual can be a useful tool in shaping staff behaviour. Its usefulness will become obvious when you need to correct or improve their performance.

5.4 The practice audit

Just as there is an annual financial audit, so too might you consider a complementary audit of the practice as a whole. There is an excellent model available in that used by the Australian Society of Certified Practising Accountants.

An accounting practice wanting such an audit obtains the services of a practice auditor. That auditor sets out the ground rules of what is to be audited (such as access to financial information, office procedures, compliance with employee legislation, Australian Securities Commission requirements and so on). The auditor is also alert to ethical issues, which include securing the permission of the accountant's clients before being given access to their files.

The outcome advantages of such an audit are that it highlights areas of strength and areas where improvement might be effected; gives an independent view of ethical and legal compliance issues; and provides an overview of the practice, which is often lost in the day-to-day running. At a more mundane level, such an audit (either by a clean bill or improved procedures) will provide a significant defence against potential or actual litigation. It will show to antagonistic parties that a genuine effort was made to operate professionally. Although an audit involves an expense, it is one expense that pays large dividends in the longer term.

5.5 Skills development

5.5.1 Business management skills

It could be argued that your success in business can really begin when you reach the point of 'knowing that you don't know'. Then and only then are you likely to start searching for ways to run a practice better and for any lack of business management skills.

Most people commence their business because they are technically good at something (at least according to their perception, which it is to be hoped accords with that of their clients). This drive and dedication are usually sufficient to get the business started. It is not until well down the track of the business development cycle that the practitioner becomes aware that to manage a practice as a business, a whole different set of skills and competencies is required.

It is helpful at this point to identify the list of desirable skills, and then seek ways to complement your own repertoire. Sometimes, simply talking to your accountant can be a deliberate attempt to learn about the financial side of managing a business. Rather than seeing the accountant for as short a time as possible you may see it as an opportunity to have someone answer your specific questions. As you are paying for it, you must really understand what you have set out to learn and not leave your accountant's office without having fulfilled your aims.

Another method is to attend various business seminars, which are so often advertised through direct mail or newsletters. You will need to select the seminars carefully to maximise the return for your investment. It is quite easy to find a seminar on marketing, or financial management, and the chances are you will learn something from each. You may also subscribe to a number of magazines, or simply buy them from the newsagents' stands, which will broaden your business horizons and possibly provide another source of valuable seminars on relevant topics. Some examples of magazines include *Professional Practice Management* and *Small Business Magazine*.

Many books on the subject of business development are also available, both in the popular and technical book stores. There are many little inspirations that can be gained from otherwise uninspiring reading for someone used to assimilating complex scientific data and arguments. One advantage of popular business books is that they are usually very easy to read. For those who are too busy to read such books, there are book summary services available on both cassette tapes and paper for a reasonable subscription fee.

The professional associations are also a useful source of information that combines both professional and practice skills and information. The APS has a Division of Independently Practising Psychologists (DIPP) with sections in each state. Some state representatives are actively promoting the development of professional practice management skills by providing seminars, displays and newsletters. Since DIPP is one of the structures of APS there is no additional charge for its membership.

An organisation devoted solely to represent the interests of private practitioners has been formed. This new body is called the Australian Psychological Association and is registered in the ACT. Private practitioners interested to know of this recently formed organisation should direct their inquiry to it directly (see Appendix A for the address).

There are other local associations that are active in promoting and supporting the psychologist in private practice, such as the Australian College of Private Consulting Psychologists (ACPCP) and its national equivalent body, the Federation of Privately Practising Psychologists of Australia (FOPPPA).

As a member of any professional association, it is up to you to define your benefit from it. Your gain will often be proportional to the level of your input. As they are voluntary organisations, they all rely on the goodwill of their members to perform most tasks. If you ever feel that 'they' are not supporting you or providing you with the required services then it is time for you to become 'them', and become active.

Like most organisations one would want there to be a reason to join. Just as many practitioners choose to belong to the APS, so do many choose not to belong. The APS is currently engaged in a survey to find out what it is that motivates people to join and to stay. That constant monitoring and responsiveness to the members' needs are a crucial part of the viability of any organisation.

5.5.2 Professional development

At the same time as you are gaining skills in practice management, you will recognise that the development of your professional knowledge and skills is paramount to your ongoing capacity to practise. Your clients depend on the knowledge and skills of you and of those you employ to provide professional services of excellent quality.

The need for your own ongoing development cannot be overemphasised. Because of your time becoming such a rare commodity when in full-time practice, you will need to become more innovative about the way you gain the extra skills. You will choose conferences and seminars selectively to provide maximum benefit. You may also choose to invest in a modem and conduct specific literature searches from your desktop computer to optimise the time you spend reading and learning.

Probably the most creative way you can enhance your practice through such targeted research is to apply the psychological body of knowledge to your practice. Many psychologists work in marketing, human factor, personnel selection and organisational fields. Their combined and published knowledge can add great value to the way you develop and manage your practice. The best ways to manage people, to motivate staff, and to select colours most likely to bring results, are all examples of fragments of psychological knowledge. To find them and to apply them will be your challenge in your quest to achieve excellence in your practice.

5.5.3 Personal development

It is surprising and incongruous that professionals providing services in the area of people development often neglect their own. Managing your practice and simultaneously working within the practice will not leave you with much spare time. You will be in charge of the vast number of activities that you will be planning, developing and executing, all at the same time. The excitement and the load that a private practice brings can easily derail your personal life. It is more important than ever to spend some time on your personal renewal.

The seventh habit of highly effective people promoted by Covey (1993) in his business management best seller is: take time to sharpen your saw. It is very much an *important but not urgent* activity. Its aim is to preserve and enhance your greatest asset — yourself. Take time to ensure that the physical, social, emotional, mental and spiritual dimensions of your life are all balanced so that you can practise for many more years to come. Some of the activities to check for are:

- exercise, breaks, holidays, nutrition and stress management;
- family time, friends and social support;
- personal security, self-esteem, excitement and laughing;
- reading for pleasure, visualising, writing and painting;
- value clarification, commitment, reflection, service study and meditation.

If you are skilled at denying that work has taken over your life while everybody else around tells you that this is so, it is easy to do a quick check by adding up the hours spent at the end of each day under the above categories (though other categories may be more applicable to you). If you find that the percentages are stacked in the work category, it is time to stop and sharpen your saw. It will be much easier and faster to use it later.

5.6 Networking

Networking with other practitioners provides vital contact to alleviate the sense of isolation. It will also help in validating and normalising your experiences. You can create formal networks around the area where you practise from, to provide easier opportunities to meet. Such networks usually provide further opportunities for informal contact as your needs arise.

Attendance at formal meetings, seminars and conferences can provide the dual benefit of gaining new skills and new network contacts. Someone has generated the following ten commandments for networking:

- Thou shalt exchange business cards.
- Thou shalt not stand in a corner.
- Thou shalt seek out and find others.
- Thou shalt make friends when they are not needed.
- Thou shalt take an interest in others.
- Thou shalt always follow up.
- Thou shalt keep in touch.
- Thou shalt act like a host, not a guest.
- Thou shalt edit thy contacts.
- Thou shalt share thy contacts.

Your encounters in various professional gatherings will increase in value if you apply these rules. Most professionals tend to network with like-minded, predictable and similar individuals, and such people provide a worthwhile support. You may find it invigorating to seek out quite a different network of individuals who will usually come from a different professional background from yourself. They may include lawyers, sales people, professional speakers or other business people. Such networks are likely to energise your thinking, challenge your vision, and therefore fulfil a different but most valuable role.

5.7 Business ethics statement

One of the telltale signs of your commitment to excellence is your practice's statement on business ethics as opposed to professional ethics.

Among the statements you might wish to consider are those that indicate to your 'consumers' that you are concerned to operate according to good explicit standards. These include:

- a mission statement of the practice — this would include the purpose of the practice (e.g. to provide high-quality reports to lawyers, or to provide professional support for victims of sexual abuse), and could also specify the mode of delivery (e.g. on an individual basis or the use of group techniques);
- a statement of the code by which they are bound (e.g. the APS Code of Professional Conduct and the Code of the Institute of Personnel Managers);
- a statement of client rights;
- a statement that privacy will be maintained except under certain specified conditions (e.g. under legal compulsion to reveal);
- your adherence to various aspects of legal compliance (such as equal opportunity employment);
- a statement on fees, how they will be calculated, when they fall due and other related matters (as outlined in Section 4.9).

A copy of these statements might be held at reception, and be available in summary form for handing to clients and potential clients when requested.

Clearly a commitment to practice ethics as well as to professional ethics are tied items. None of this will matter one iota if the commitment is not genuine — the consuming public have strong inbuilt sincerity detectors. While statements such as we have suggested are really useful, their existence must be matched by good-spirited implementation. For example, no matter how good a statement on fees is made, it is how a complicated situation is handled that will determine your client's view of your operation.

Listening and negotiating are preferable to pointing to inflexible 'rules'. People from the most diverse backgrounds object to the same issues: firmly located here are the twin complaints of 'no one ever told me' and 'no one ever asked me'. While you have professional and ethical principles that you will maintain, so too do we recommend that explaining, seeking common ground and listening sympathetically are part of the process of implementing your standards. See also Francis (1994) for information on business ethics.

6
Expanding your practice

Once your practice has passed through the stage of 'getting organised', and has developed business systems that ensure you can deliver services with consistent quality, you might desire to reach the stage of 'maturity'. In this phase, the business systems work well, they get constantly tuned, the clients are satisfied and you are not overworked.

It might seem somewhat utopian but it is true for many organisations. If you find it hard to believe that it is possible not to be overworked and still run a successful practice, this chapter has been written to show you how.

The paradox of being successful in private practice, or any business for that matter, is that the better you are, the more in demand you are. The greater the demand, the worse you become, and your personal life could suffer so much that you will wonder if business success is really worth it.

You may react to this demand differently and begin to think of expansion. You have so much work so why not share it with others. You could identify the areas where you need help such as administration or practice management, counselling, training or consulting, and try to find someone with any of these capabilities. To put this another way — delegate: and do so for those functions that others with appropriate skills can readily perform.

It is even more manageable if you have already developed the business and quality systems discussed in Chapter 5. This additional person would find it relatively easy to apply the system as laid out in the operations manual. Induction training would also be so much easier if the new staff member in your practice could read the manual rather than learning it personally from you.

Quite often at this stage of practice development there is a real fear about employing someone, and being responsible for getting work for someone else. If this type of thinking is crippling your decision making, there are other ways of expanding your practice than by employing people. These will be explored below. Such a fear needs to be overcome if you are ever going to be freed from the tyranny of simultaneously being the practice and running the practice.

If someone else comes into the practice you will have to share this identity. When you market your practice, it will no longer be just you being promoted. What you will promote is a business that provides a professional service and it may be actually provided by someone else — your staff.

6.1 Staffing

6.1.1 Recognising the need

The decision to employ administrative staff rather than professional staff is usually made earlier in the development phase. Initially you may take on all roles in the practice by yourself. Because your time is not translated into money and you have little of it to invest, it is easier to wear many hats yourself. You might say: 'It does not cost me anything'. This could well be a reasonable approach initially but you must become aware of the moment when the lost opportunity of your time's real financial worth prevents the business from growing and freeing you up, through its growth, to achieve your life goals.

Some highly successful practices identify the moment when they employed the first person they could not afford, as the turning point in their financial performance and their best business decision. The reason for this turnaround was that they were forced to do more marketing and spend more time in the professional role, thus earning much more for the practice. Then the true value of their previously lost earning opportunity became obvious. *The more time you spend on bookkeeping, typing and writing invoices the less time you have to earn income.* Hunger becomes a very powerful motivation to earn more income.

The recognition that you need assistance with professional work usually comes later. It may occur perhaps for the first time when you are about to plan your next holiday only to realise that your business gets in the way. If you go away for a number of weeks who will look after your practice, answer phones and see clients when needed? The compromise may be to take a few short breaks, so that your clients never really miss you. While away you check your phone messages, or receive them regularly through your pager system. You may feel the need to respond to them, so you get on the mobile phone and . . . you are back at work. While this may work for a while, you will probably realise deep within that it cannot last for too long. Your independent practice all of a sudden shows few signs of flexibility and independence — your main aims for starting it in the first place. It has become too dependent on you, and you have become imprisoned by it.

The need for professional assistance may also be experienced sporadically: when the work increases for a period of time, or when you may be involved in a specific short-term project. It may last for only a few weeks, and it becomes quite obvious that you cannot carry out all the tasks yourself. Some projects may involve assessments of a large number of employees, and the time frames are impossible to meet by one practitioner. This is another point of business decision making. You can either contract the work out to someone else, form a temporary alliance with another practice, or employ someone on a full-time, part-time or casual basis. If you choose the latter option or if you have already recognised the need for administrative, reception and book-keeping assistance, you will have no option but to accept your new identity in life — you will now be an employer.

6.1.2 Fundamentals of employer–employee relationship

There are well-established characteristics defining the relationship between employer and employee, the fundamental one being that the employer pays employees for the work performed. This important transaction gives rise to many expectations on both sides. The employee's livelihood becomes dependent on the employer, and there is an expectation of needing to be looked after. The employer parts with hard-earned money and has an expectation that the employees will behave according to his or her instructions. This relationship is particularly evident in small organisations where the exertion of its few members generates the majority of its income.

All too often some of these expectations are not entirely met to everyone's satisfaction. The employee may ask for more money, more leave entitlements or special treatment for compassionate reasons. The employer may demand that the tasks are performed in a different or better way. While this chapter is not meant to be a treatise on employee relations and human resource management there has to be a clear recognition on the part of practice owners that they are subject to all the rules and regulations governing employer and employee relationship. Having become an employer you must behave like one.

6.1.3 Employer responsibilities

Becoming an employer carries with it numerous responsibilities, which must be taken seriously. The fear of responsibilities being too onerous should not prevent you from becoming an employer as the potential benefits far outweigh the problems associated with this new identity.

One of the first tasks will be to register your practice as a group employer with the Australian Taxation Office. You will be allocated an employer number and will be sent all the relevant details about your responsibilities in relation to taxation.

Remuneration

One of the most obvious functions the employer must perform is to ensure that the employee is adequately rewarded for effort. The wages and salaries are governed by various state or federal awards, which you may easily obtain by contacting the appropriate government departments or by phoning or faxing Wage Help lines. You may wish to obtain a copy of the entire award, either from the relevant government department, employer association, chamber of commerce or a union.

Apart from agreeing on the hourly rate, you need to agree on the frequency and the basis on which remuneration will be paid (e.g. weekly or fortnightly, by cheque or direct credit into the bank, and which day of the week pay will be distributed). Irrespective of whether pay is delivered by cheque or through a direct bank transaction, you will need to provide employees with their pay advice slip, showing clearly how their amount of pay was calculated.

Irrespective of the number of people on your staff, you will need to manage the overall payroll function, which means keeping the records of paid amounts, taxation details, all entitlements and superannuation. The most cost-efficient method for small numbers of staff is to keep a manual record of every pay. There are specially prepared forms for this purpose, which you purchase from office stationery suppliers and some newsagents.

There are a number of different bases for rewarding people for their work, including the following:

- Regular salary is calculated on an hourly basis, either full-time, part-time (with the set number of hours each week), or casual (variable number of hours each week). The casual rates have built-in compensation for public holidays and leave entitlements, and so these hourly rates tend to be higher (at least 15%). The higher cost of wages is balanced by having no cost associated with sick leave and annual leave.
- Regular salary plus performance-based bonus would necessitate a very clearly defined system for determining the amount and timing of bonuses. For example, for support staff, the bonus arrangement could be an amount calculated on an annual basis, and would depend on the level of their performance as measured by some predefined indicators; for professional staff, the bonus could be a regular extra payment in each pay period calculated on the basis of the time charged out to clients.
- Another basis is a commission-based contract. These hourly rates must be much higher than the regular hourly rates (at least twice if not three times the normal wage rate). This basis of payment is applicable only to professional staff who are able to generate income through their work and involves payment for the time that was actually charged out by the practice; hence the need for a higher pay rate to compensate the person for all the other work that is not chargeable such as writing reports, administration and marketing.

Note, however, that this type of employment should not be confused with a co-practice partnership type arrangement, which is discussed in Section 6.1.5 under the heading 'Co-practice arrangements'. If the person is employed on a contract basis that person is primarily your employee, not another psychologist in private practice.

- A combination of the above methods may be used, where either a regular salary rate or a contract rate applies, plus an additional annual bonus system that is defined on the basis of the overall practice's financial performance.

Employee entitlements

Employee leave entitlements include sick, annual and long service leave, and may include family, compassionate, maternity, paternity and special leave. While these are not actually paid each week, your accounting procedures may need to reflect the liability that your practice is accruing during the period of employment. This may not be necessary if the amounts are small, as your accountant may advise. When they are substantial or when you need to show an accurate balance sheet you will need to present all kinds of liability that you have accrued. These include staff-related overheads that will have to be paid even if the person is not at work. A point of caution here is the way in which entitlements might build up. For example, you do not want to suddenly find yourself liable to send a valued employee on 3 months' long service leave — on full pay. You deprive yourself of a key staff member and need to find the money to pay them — and to pay their replacement.

To illustrate the need for staff policies, you may need to determine whether an employee should be paid a leave entitlement before fully accruing it. After what period of employment will your staff be able to claim their entitlement for sick leave or annual leave? Is sick leave accumulative? How long is long service? Can sick leave be used when a family member needs care?

The answers to these questions are not difficult — they just require attention to detail. It may well be most efficient to write down as many rules as you can think of, from the days when you were in the employee's position and when others in personnel and human resource departments were making such rules for you. Then deal with each exception to the rules as it comes up, and keep adding to your staff policy as you become aware of its limitations.

Taxation

Probably the most serious responsibility of employers is to pay PAYE (pay as you earn) tax on behalf of the employee to the Australian Taxation Office. Employers have an obligation to deduct the correct amount of tax from each gross pay, put aside this amount in their account and pay the group tax on a monthly or quarterly basis, carefully following the instructions laid out in the group employer information kit. Late payments of any tax liabilities are heavily and immediately penalised.

Correct information needs to be obtained from the employee at commencement of employment with regard to tax file numbers and other special additional tax obligations, such as the Higher Education Contribution Scheme (HECS) or child support.

At the end of the year the employer must present the accurate group certificate to each employee. Even those who might have worked for a few days only or on special projects need to receive their group certificate as soon as possible after the end of financial year — 30 June.

The obligation to take group tax out of the gross pay also applies to those engaged on a contract basis, unless there is no employer–employee relationship between the contractor and your psychology practice. There has been much confusion and ambiguity in this area and it is likely to continue. There are some well-known litmus tests of this relationship, which you can apply to your situation to determine whether or not you need to take tax out of someone's pay. If contractors are essentially under your control as employees would be, and if these contractors work exclusively in your practice, there is little doubt they are your employees. Another way to determine the relationship is whether you pay the contractors regularly on the basis of their time spent in your practice or on presentation of an invoice. In other words, are the contractors really in business by themselves, and can they demonstrate this, maintaining their own equipment and such like? Payments on an invoice are mostly irregular and short term, for example a contractor computer expert who comes in for a few hours as need arises.

This is an important issue to clarify in the development of your staff policy, because there is a tendency for contractor-employees to prefer to pay their own tax, and the corresponding preference for the employer not to pay the group tax to avoid the extra administrative burden. Since these personal preferences tend in the same direction it is easy to reach consensus when the employer and the prospective contractor negotiate their employment conditions. Such consensus is not always right and you, the employer, have greater penalties to fear and more to lose, if you do not comply with the employer's taxation regulations. It is recommended that you always seek advice from your accountant, an employer association or a relevant government body when in doubt and, preferably, in writing.

While on the topic of taxation regulations, it is a good practice to behave in all your financial decisions and record keeping as though you were expecting a taxation audit. Such audits are more commonplace now, and it is better to be prepared than surprised. One way to prepare for such an eventuality is to ask your external accountant to conduct a pre-audit once every few years. This may also provide an opportunity to improve your business systems, and lead to greater efficiencies in your practice administration. The employer must keep the record of each employee for 7 years from when the record originated, or from the time of the employment being terminated.

Finally, it also makes sense to make provision for your own provisional tax, if it applies to you. This is tax paid *ahead* in the expectation of the tax for which you will be liable, if you earn any income that has not already been taxed throughout the year. If you are an employer, one way to minimise the impact of paying tax in lump sums is to pay yourself a salary as an employee (and therefore tax as well), on a regular basis throughout the year. Do ask your accountant for advice.

Superannuation

The employer's responsibilities have recently included a compulsory superannuation payment to a fund nominated by the employee. Unless employees begin their working career at your practice, they are likely to have an existing fund from the previous place of employment. This payment is currently set at 5% of salary, and under current regulations will increase to 9% by the year 2000. The superannuation payment must be made on a regular basis as determined by the trust deed of the employee's fund.

Workers' compensation

As a group employer you have an obligation to cover your staff for workers' compensation insurance. At this stage, state governments control this area and most of them do so through WorkCover legislation and authorities. The amount of WorkCover premium is calculated on the basis of your practice's total remuneration amount and the relevant industry grouping.

Depending on your state or territory regulations and the number of employees in your practice you may also have certain obligations in the area of rehabilitation, such as a policy and a return-to-work program. This needs to be prominently displayed. Some WorkCover regulations also require that employers display information about how to claim for compensation and maintain an injury record. It is recommended that you familiarise yourself with such regulations.

Insurance

In the case of employing professional staff, you will need to cover their insurance for malpractice liability, professional indemnity, legal expenses and public liability. As previously mentioned, the relevant professional associations (e.g. APS) have very favourable arrangements with insurance underwriters to provide policies and premiums for individual members. Such policies become quite expensive when you as an employer have to cover a number of individuals in your practice. You may find it much more cost efficient to obtain a group liability cover through an insurance broker.

It may be one of the conditions of employment that your employees are responsible for their own professional indemnity insurance cover. You need to be mindful that some organisations seeking your services will require proof of your professional indemnity and public liability insurance, and they may further nominate a certain level of cover. An example of such a demand is a contract for the provision of an employee assistance program (EAP), or a training needs analysis project to a government organisation. It may be unreasonable to demand that each individual employee carries such levels of cover to fulfil the contractual obligations to which your practice is party. Furthermore, if your employees are covered personally for professional indemnity and public insurance, you will still need to assure yourself that their policies are current to ensure that you are not in breach of the contract.

Seeking assistance about employer's obligations

The above brief discussion of employment issues is only a very general and partial introduction to the long evolving industrial relations law and practice in Australia. There are many other decisions you will be called to make as an employer that are subject to a plethora of legislation covering employee issues. A wrong decision can be very costly. On the other hand, a decision to employ the right person can be most rewarding to your business.

Other issues, occurring less often but nevertheless having serious potential impact, are termination, contract of employment, enterprise bargaining, union representation, dishonesty, procedural and substantive fairness of dismissal, equal opportunity, sexual harassment, occupational health and safety, and workplace contracts, to name just a few.

It is best to seek professional advice when in doubt, and make yourself aware of the current legislation and employer obligations at all times. The useful sources of such advice are:

- employer associations (such as a chamber of commerce);
- your accountant or solicitor;
- the Australian Taxation Office;
- the federal Department of Industrial Relations (DIR) and its publications;
- the state/territory departments responsible for industrial relations;
- periodical publications that are offered by numerous information-based businesses, either in hard copy or on a computer disk (such as the Wicks annual update of federal legislation).

A list of contact addresses and phone numbers is provided in Appendix B. In general, four principles are recommended for sound employment practice (DIR, 1995):

- *Be informed* Keep updating your knowledge in this area and take it seriously.
- *Be fair* Act in a way that recognises mutual personal rights.
- *Think ahead* Plan, document your employment policies and inform all employees.
- *Keep good records* Document the basis for all your decisions and comply with the financial record-keeping requirements.

6.1.4 Employing support staff

Employing support staff is usually a simple decision that most full-time practices embrace at an early point in their development. The most common experience consists of the employment of one person who shares the tasks in the following areas:

- reception (e.g. telephone answering, making appointments and handling client reception);
- office administration (filing and so on);
- typing or word processing;
- client data maintenance (either manual or computer based);
- invoicing clients; and
- following up unpaid debt.

Bookkeeping and paying accounts can also be included in the same person's role, providing it does not place unreasonable demands on that person's time and skills. This scenario usually involves compilation of the documents that are forwarded to the external accountant. The accountant usually provides a quarterly or, maybe, a yearly financial statement.

Another and perhaps more cost-effective approach in a larger practice is to employ a dedicated person, most likely on a part-time basis, to manage the accounting function in house. Apart from managing all accounts payable, the in-house bookkeeper will also be in charge of payroll function, which will lessen the burden on the practice owners involved with personnel administrative issues.

6.1.5 Employing professionals

Employing a professional to perform some of the services that you probably perform yourself carries with it much more risk, and is usually shunned by practitioners. Such a professional needs to represent you and your practice. In many respects your practice will depend on the competence, commitment and integrity of the professional — as it has on yours.

While the risk is there you need to simply be more careful when selecting such a person. It is possible to locate highly competent and trustworthy individuals who prefer to be employed rather than running practices. They might just be the ones who, having read the second chapter of this book, have decided that their enterprising interest and skill are not adequate to embark on this journey. There is no universal truth in the popular belief that if you are really good then you will be working for yourself.

If you wish to embark on employing professionals within your practice you would be prudent to take the task of recruiting and selecting extremely seriously, and to proceed with caution. When you have found the right person you might just discover that you do not need to turn into a salesperson to constantly find jobs or clients for your new employee. Such professionals will probably be acutely aware of their need to charge far more than they earn to ensure their job viability.

If you are not prepared to take such a step, and you have a need for professional assistance in your practice because of the volume of work, there are other options that are explored below.

Co-practice arrangements

Some practitioners feel most comfortable with the scenario where the new co-professional shares maximum responsibility for marketing and finding new clients. Your dilemma is that your practice has already earned its reputation and developed its image. To the extent that it already has a defined product and a market, the invited new professional should find it easier to market his or her services than you did originally. This, in a sense, is the value of goodwill.

Common mistakes that are often made at this point consist of either giving away too much or of overestimating the goodwill. If you are in the former category, you will essentially enter into a belated partnership arrangement where everything is shared equally. If you fall into the latter error, you will underpay the prospective co-practitioner and expect that person to be a partner. Our experience seems to suggest that there are more cases in the latter category.

You must not forget that in this expansion scenario you are not entering into an employer–employee relationship, and so it is inappropriate to set a salary rate. The co-practitioner should be left to set his or her own fees, and your practice instead should charge for the services that it provides to the new practitioner.

The first component of such a fee is the administration and reception support. If your practice has such facilities and the new professional makes full use of them, the situation is parallel to that of a serviced office. The value of such services can therefore be easily benchmarked against such commercially available facilities. Essentially, a rent fee can be set, depending on the level of support provided.

The second and most contentious component is related to marketing. If your co-practitioner gains clients through his or her own marketing effort, the co-practitioner is entitled to a reasonably large percentage of the charged fee. The co-practitioner needs to be compensated for the time spent on marketing activities, as you would have expected in your practice. If, on the other hand, the new professional simply works with the existing clients of your practice, the relationship with you becomes more like that of an employee and employer. There may be a reasonable argument for a marketing levy applied to your co-practitioner for every chargeable hour in such cases, in addition to the rent and support fee.

This is a rather complicated scenario but it is nevertheless frequently entered into by many practitioners, desperate to gain assistance with their work but not willing to become an employer. If such an option is being considered, it is recommended instead to apply a partnership model more formally, by entering into properly constructed contracts. Be alert to being responsible for all partnership debts if your partner avoids them. There are other examples of such models operating most successfully, notably in the legal profession. It is best to call such relationships what they really are — partnerships — and structure them accordingly.

Contractor and locum arrangement

Another common scenario is that the practitioner enters into a temporary arrangement with another psychologist who becomes a locum or a short-term contractor. The precipitating events are usually a large temporary workload, or a holiday or other prolonged absence of the practice owner.

It is the best response to the short-term need, so that your practice can truly meet your life goals, which almost certainly should not include being tied to consulting rooms at all times. This scenario is very much like a short-term employment contract and needs to be developed as such. Because contractors will not enjoy the usual job tenure and employee entitlements, they should be compensated by a much greater hourly rate than full-time employees. To start negotiations we suggest 50% of the charged fee. For this contractors would bear considerable responsibility — both professional and reputational. If this works well both sides are in front. If it does not work well, some business will be lost to the owner — and serious reputational damage will be done to the temporary incumbent.

If remuneration is totally commission based, that is, contractors are paid just for the hours you can charge, their fee will depend on the amount of time you expect them to spend on non-chargeable activities. If they simply turn up to see your clients, and charge for almost every hour they spend at work, this fee could justifiably be quite low (say, double the salary rate, to compensate them for loss of normal entitlements). If, on the other hand, you expect them to run your practice for you, and perform a large amount of non-chargeable activities, their remuneration should rise accordingly (say, up to four times their salary rate).

As with the co-practice the principle of fairness must apply between employers and employees, partners, principals and colleagues — just as it does in all other areas of life. When dealing with partners or with co-practitioners, equity should be maintained. To ensure this there are some practical questions that one might ask: Who carries the financial risk? Who puts in the professional time? Whose reputation is at risk? How is marketing time to be costed as a contribution? What is the value of a client base, and how is its contribution to be estimated? There are some fundamental rules that prevent resentment: among these are the firm commitment to equal contributions and equal risks. The person who is exposed to more risk should also expect better rewards.

The potential disappointments from such short-term relationships can be easily prevented by setting expectations before the relationship starts. All tasks should be documented as in the job description for the employee (see Section 6.1.6).

Below are some of the questions that should be addressed and documented by both contractors and employing practitioners before starting the contract:

- When does a contractor get paid?
- On what basis is the payment calculated: per chargeable session, per any session, per hour, per week?
- What are the exact dollar rates involved?
- What is expected regarding note keeping and writing reports?
- What is expected regarding accounting records (e.g. telephone calls, number of sessions and activities)?
- Who is responsible for professional indemnity insurance?
- Who is responsible for workers' compensation insurance?
- Is the contractor entitled to any paid leave (sick leave, annual leave and so on)?
- Who is responsible for the marketing of the practice?
- What arrangements apply if the contractor develops clearly defined clientele for the practice?
- What is expected to occur at the termination of the contract, particularly in relation to clients who choose to continue with the contractor and new clients/contracts gained as a direct result of the contract employment, and to records and other intellectual property?
- What is the duration of the contract?
- What undertakings are needed to prevent poaching of clients?

- Is there an embargo on the temporary incumbent practising in the same field of psychology, or within a nominated geographical location or for a fixed period of time?

6.1.6 Job description

Whatever the employment contract and whatever job is involved, support or professional, there are some basic principles to follow to increase the productivity of employees and their usefulness to the practice.

The first of these is planning a job before the person is recruited and selected. You must first identify what the job consists of and what sort of person would best fit the tasks. Such planning requires that you document all the tasks in a job description or a duty statement. Such a document will include at least:

- job name;
- date of last update;
- tasks;
- level of accountability;
- supervisory arrangements;
- measures of satisfactory job performance;
- prerequisite qualifications; and
- minimum knowledge, skills and attitude.

The last two items are of particular use during the selection process. They will form the selection criteria.

6.1.7 Selection and placement

It is probably true that you realise how vital the task of recruiting and selecting the right person is only when you have experienced placing the wrong person. The amount of unproductive time and the potential damage to a business suffered by such an error is of such proportions that virtually any amount of investment in a thorough selection process will never be too much.

A well-constructed job description will be the basis for developing useful selection criteria, which will in turn be related to the tasks. You may consider some tests, which may be quite appropriate in the setting of psychology practice. You will then employ the well-used selection interview technique. Its effectiveness can be drastically increased if you plan to structure it in such a way that each key selection criterion is well represented in your questions. A structured interview uses behaviourally based questions as much as possible, and the same questions are applied to every applicant. Ideally, you should interview in a panel so that more opinions can be gathered. The candidates' performance is tested systematically against each criterion.

By following the selection process as systematically as you feel you can handle it, rather than relying totally on your intuition and interviewing skills, you are likely to improve the probability of a hit. We are well aware of the poor validity of interviewing as a selection technique — but we do subscribe to the view that it is a much better system for rejecting an inappropriate applicant.

In this personnel selection system, which you will have developed in your practice to reach for excellence, you will also want to ensure that all references or referees are followed up without fail. A second interview may also be appropriate.

Once you have made an offer of employment it is a sound practice to confirm it by sending a letter, which would include at least the following:

- date and time of expected commencement;
- the place of employment;
- the duration of the trial period;
- the remuneration details, including review systems;
- supervisory structure; and
- the summary of major areas of involvement.

You should not forget that some of the other applicants who missed out on a job may be your future clients, in some capacity. Even if they were never to become your clients, the image of your practice needs to be consistently communicated to everyone around you. Whether and what you write to the unsuccessful applicants, and how long you take to write to them, will also send them a message about your practice and your professionalism. This will happen whether you intended it or not.

6.1.8 Induction training

Once the selection has been made and the person placed in a job, the area of training must also be addressed. Whatever other training the person will undertake, the initial induction will determine, to a large extent, his or her compliance with your practice system. Rather than relying on informal chat as the person turns up for the first day, it is far more effective to have the induction process structured. Your operations manual, discussed in Chapter 5, will now turn into a most useful document that can provide a structure to your induction training.

An induction session is an excellent opportunity to instil in the employee the values of your practice and the philosophy underpinning your approach to business. It is also the ideal time to introduce your practice's vision and mission statements as well as its ethics, which will govern the behaviour of all involved in your practice.

The practice manual should not be long or complex in its approach. It should provide new employees with a clear knowledge of your expectations of them. It will inform them of how their performance is measured and reviewed.

6.1.9 Performance review

The process of performance and development reviews is a familiar concept to all who have worked in large organisations. Unfortunately, to many the memory of it is often stained with bureaucratic procedures and little effective change. This is unfortunate because psychologists know well how feedback, when used appropriately, can become a powerful tool in gaining new skills and shaping someone's behaviour. While the concept of regular performance reviews is potentially the best strategy towards increasing the employee's effectiveness, its application has led many organisations to ineffectual results.

The other psychological concept that performance review designers heavily rely on is goal setting. The entire review process revolves around setting realistic, *measurable* goals for your employee's behaviour, developed with the employee's full participation, and then giving regular and frequent feedback with regard to the achievement of those goals.

Some of the outcomes from the reviews may have to do with the skill development of the person, which has been identified as the reason for the gap between the expected and actual performance. If you agreed for the employee to attend a relevant training course, for example, you need to follow it through and pay for it, when the time comes. Your failure to do so can seriously undermine the value of the whole process.

You can also use the review process to gain insight into your management style by requesting that the employee provides you with an honest appraisal of your performance in this area. If you are able to suppress your ego defensive mechanisms at such reviews, these sessions can be useful opportunities to improve yourself and your practice.

Your formal system of performance reviews does not mean that you disregard the everyday feedback and ongoing informal interaction with your employee. You can at the same time be a 'one minute manager' who helps people reach their full potential by 'catching them doing something right'. The immediacy of feedback should also form part of your management repertoire (Blanchard & Johnson, 1982).

6.2 Marketing

As you have now expanded the practice by employing more staff, the issue of marketing will probably return to the fore in your thinking; that is, if it ever went away, since marketing is ongoing. You may even dream ideas and network at a social barbeque when you least expect it. You will always have your business cards with you, just in case someone asks you about what you do and sounds interested.

You will need to exercise obvious caution when involving your social networks in the marketing of your practice. First, you need to be careful not to alienate your friends and their contacts; and, second, you may face ethical dilemmas when providing services to those to whom you are socially related. Keeping these restrictions in mind there are still plenty of opportunities to find potential business leads in everyday interactions with people.

Ideally, the marketing strategy, which will form part of your business plan (see Section 3.4), will now be in place and in its implementation phase. Your initial marketing will have also taken place to inform the world around about the arrival of your practice on the market (see Section 4.7). But now you need more ideas to give your practice an extra boost so that you can guarantee some stability of income not just for yourself but also for the people you now employ or contract. This section provides you with some practical ideas that you can use in your future revised marketing strategy.

In your approach to marketing you need to be aware of the long-term nature of its coming to fruition. Quite often, particularly in the corporate market, ideas that you have communicated through your brochure, letter or a speaking engagement may not produce any outcomes for a number of months or years. Some, of course, will never lead to positive outcomes. You should not expect immediate results, particularly when the marketing activity aims at creating a higher profile. Instead, it is helpful to think that your marketing efforts of today will have their effect in a year's time. This simple recognition will lead you to actively market at times when you are very busy, even though it seems counter-intuitive, so that you can continue to be busy in the future.

6.2.1 Speaking engagements

One of the easiest ways to become known in the local, corporate or professional community is through offering your public speaking services. Depending on the situation, you can either charge for it or deliver it free. For example, a local school or a health community centre may need someone to conduct a parenting skills seminar or a session on learning skills for the students. A local dietitian or a medical practice may be interested in conducting public sessions on eating disorders. The opportunities are limited only by your imagination. To expand it a little, start by asking them about the need for public seminars in your area.

In the corporate market, there are numerous conferences and training seminars whose organisers search for credible, knowledgeable and obviously high-quality speakers on all sorts of management and people-related subjects from occupational stress to family friendly policies. Such conference papers are expected to be delivered free of charge, although the organisers may contribute towards your travel and accommodation costs. There are also many formal associations that organise conferences and training seminars at which speaking engagements are sought. Some of these are listed in Appendix A for your reference.

Before attempting this strategy you need to be confident in your presentation skills and in your message. You need to have something interesting and captivating to say and it is essential that you deliver this message well.

You are advised to first research the topic in depth, to be sure that you can claim to be the expert in it. To test your public speaking skills you may first practise your delivery in the feedback-giving atmosphere of a club concerned with public speaking, such as Toastmasters, Rostrum or the National Speakers' Association. We strongly recommend the section on delivering a talk in Sternberg's (1993) book.

Following a well-attended presentation it is not uncommon for some people, to whom your message was particularly relevant, to approach you personally. You will need to have your business cards handy to give out. To maximise the effectiveness of your presentation for marketing purposes, ask other people first for their card or contact details. Once you know who they are, you can follow them up.

6.2.2 Writing articles

A similar principle is that of writing articles or books on the subject of your expertise. Books can add considerably to your reputation, if well done. They will do significantly more so if they are produced to proper professional standards by a reputable publisher; they are well reviewed in journals or magazines that your potential clients read; and there is seen to be some practical outcome of your special knowledge. When these conditions are satisfied the beneficial publicity is connected to a sometimes undeserved reputation for being a national expert. At the United Nations, there is a saying that an expert is someone who has overflown the country at least once, and an international expert is someone who has flown over it *in daylight*. Notwithstanding these comments, there is no doubt that a good book will enhance your reputation: it will also add to your knowledge and understanding in a way that few other experiences can match.

Books take considerable time to plan, a long time to write and an age in production. A quicker learning route is to write articles. Unless your paper or article is of stunning significance its appearance in a psychology journal is unlikely to have a beneficial short-term outcome. To this end you might consider writing for more secular forums. If you are in business psychology, writing for business or personnel magazines has much to commend it; if you are in educational psychology, another publication outlet is appropriate. We have been repeatedly struck by the diffuse effects of reputation: the 'I have heard of you before' statement.

Unless the hearing was grossly detrimental it does convey the impression of being well known and well regarded. Articles that are excellently written, and make one or two points, are always in demand. In many cases they will identify you and your practice. Nothing beats having a good article published, for which you are paid as well (being paid to advertise your practice is a benefit that is hard to beat).

6.2.3 Public media

You do not need to have lots of money to get into the public news media: television, radio and newspapers. To use these media to your advantage you will need to understand how they operate. The information you would like to publicise must be newsworthy. This will be different for different media. For example, to a local paper your practice opening may be a news item. For television your news item has to have a much wider appeal.

If you have become a prominent figure through a public presentation to a seminar or a conference you may be approached for an interview. You must be prepared and skilled for a live interview to be sure that you will gain rather than lose from the experience. (The APS, 1995, has published *Effective Media Techniques* guide for this purpose.) You may find it worthwhile to attend various media workshops offered by trainers and those held at professional conferences.

Media appearances can be beneficial if well done. Here the risks are considerable. The electronic media, in particular, go for the quick grab. The brevity of the point and the editing of its presentation carry a serious risk of being misunderstood. Failure to carry a good message to your potential clients may be compounded by a matching disparagement of your competence and probity as determined by your peers. As mentioned in *The Professional Psychology Handbook*, you do not want to be seen as a triple A person (talk on Anything, Anywhere, Anytime). That risk also attaches to being a talkback show psychologist. If it were that easy why would a serious professional spend so long doing the job, and with moderate success, if it could be done in 3 minutes without even seeing the person? The medium may convey the wrong message.

If there is any prospect of media contact we must strongly urge you to read and remember the Code of Ethics of the Australian Journalists' Association. It is in *The Professional Psychology Handbook*. It will provide you with both insight and useful defensive material.

6.2.4 Voluntary work

Another strategy of raising one's profile is to do some worthy professional work for no fee. Your local school, your local municipality or some worthy service club could well use your talents. The amount of unpaid work done in Australia out of generosity of spirit would, if paid, add considerably to the national debt. Doing such work is a way of paying something back to society for the benefits that we enjoy, and fills the heart even if it does not fill the pocket. One cannot predict the business benefits that might flow from such charitable work — but at worst one will have done something constructive and worthwhile, as well as having improved a personal reputation.

6.2.5 Client newsletters

After your personal marketing effort of visiting your organisational clients and the referrers of your individual clients, you can continually remind them of your existence. One way to do so is always to respond to a referral by writing a 'thank you' letter, and continuing to keep in touch with the referrer.

This can take place only if you have received a referral. You must also remind those who have not referred anyone that your services and your practice still exist. A useful way of achieving this is through a regular (e.g. quarterly or monthly) client newsletter. You would need to ensure that articles are well researched and written in a journalistic style to maximise its readability. If the expense of such a newsletter is prohibitive, your professional association or your informal network may be able to organise a collective project.

A special format of a newsletter could be a cassette tape, on which you can record a useful but short message about a particular topic that will be of relevance to the receiver. For example, it could be a few stress management tips or a personal development series.

6.2.6 Relationship marketing

As your newsletter or any other communication reaches your client, there is often a positive response: 'I have been meaning to call you'. This becomes particularly obvious when you follow up your potential client or project referrers personally by phone. The discussion then develops around the area of need they have. As you do so, you may wonder what would have happened had you not called. The answer is probably, in most cases, nothing. Unless the need is pressing, most people tend to spend time in their urgent activities, and your services do not fall into this category.

As you follow up your potential sources of work on a regular basis the relationships will inevitably develop, even if they are telephone based. Many successful sales people refer to their concept of selling as relationship based. They learn so much about their customers that they can anticipate their needs. Selling them a service or product becomes much easier if you understand in what way this product will benefit them.

To fully gain from this approach you will first need to keep records on the various bits of information you have collected about them in your many conversations over the years. Second, and more important, you must be genuinely interested in them as people, and approach this professional relationship in such a way that their needs will become more important to you. Otherwise, your relationship based on intention to sell will be very short lived or at least very unproductive.

6.2.7 Developing tangible psychology products

One of the problems of marketing psychology is that its services are not tangible and not easily understood by our society in general. To influence you, the reader, in this area this book has been referring to psychology products. To be more effective in your practice marketing strategy, it helps to make your services as tangible as possible.

You can turn a generic counselling service into a tangible product by focusing on one aspect, giving it a specific name, calling it a program and producing a brochure about it. You can further add to its tangibility by producing a series of cassette tapes or a manual to explain how the counselling is to be used. This process is known as 'branding', that is, providing a recognisable brand name for your product.

You can even 'tangibilise' a general counselling session by providing the individual client with a report on your diagnosis, including a chart of test results and outlining a proposed course of intervention. By the client walking out of your practice with a piece of paper, you already have added tangibility to your service. The use of biofeedback in therapy, for example, performs that additional function.

6.2.8 Direct mail

When your services become products you can market them more effectively through direct mail. It is important to identify your target market really well before attempting a direct mail campaign. There are many catalogues of lists of names that can guide you in finding the right group. The *List of Lists* is a publication providing a comprehensive database of all readily available lists of target groups, and it is available through Australia Post. You can also obtain a marked reduction in postal charges if you apply for a discount with your local post office, which is available for the distribution of advertising materials.

Marketing professionals have worked out that the most consistent results come from the classic three-piece mailing, consisting of a letter, brochure and response card. Personalised letters tend to do better than those addressed to 'The Manager' or in any other impersonal way. A letter with a PS, urging the receiver to respond, tends to outsell one without. Typing the receiver's address on the response card brings better results than do labels, and heavy, quality stock envelopes outperform lighter and cheaper ones.

Above all, you first have to ensure that you are sending information to a potential client who is interested in this information and needs the product you are selling.

6.2.9 Telemarketing

One of the best ways to increase the results from your direct mail is to engage telemarketing service providers. They follow up the recipients of your direct mail information and usually make appointments for you to see them. If your product is easily understood and tangible they could even finalise sales — to a training seminar, for example, or a cassette tape series.

This sort of marketing is mostly applicable to the sorts of programs that you can more easily sell on the phone, although your personal visits, which will be organised by your telemarketers, can also achieve a further result if the phone call did not.

6.2.10 Advertising

Your services can be advertised in newspapers, electronic media or relevant directories. Refer to the discussion on advertising at the initial set-up (Section 4.7); the same rules and ideas apply when expanding the practice. Review the statements of the APS Code of Professional Conduct in relation to public announcements and advertising, and comply with them.

Apart from announcing your practice, advertising works well when you have a specific product — the more tangible the better. It serves either to increase the profile of your practice or to promote a specific program or service.

6.2.11 Internet home pages

A more innovative way to introduce your services is by a home page on the Internet. While it is relatively inexpensive at the moment, its target market is quite uncertain but it obviously includes computer-literate people. If your services lend themselves to this sort of advertising, you may consider having a home page professionally developed, which will increase its readability. It is possible to place a counter on it to check the number of visits to your web site.

6.3 Tenders and contracts

A source of potential work is found in tenders called by corporate and government organisations. While these are often associated with building and other trades, they also apply to all kinds of professional services.

6.3.1 How to apply

Tenders are essentially requests for competitive quotations for specifically defined projects or services, such as employee counselling or training needs analyses. Closed tenders are those where the requesting organisation preselects a number of competing service providers and writes to them directly, seeking their submissions in the form of an Expression of Interest or a Specific Proposal. Open tenders are usually advertised widely through all kinds of media outlets and anyone can apply to provide the required services.

It is normally accepted that the requesting organisation prepares a Consultants' Brief, which outlines the requirements. You should always obtain this document and any relevant information before submitting your document. If the brief calls for Expressions of Interest, it is a preliminary call for your credentials and experience in the relevant field. It is usually a precursor to a call for Proposals. If you are submitting a Proposal, it will normally need to include your approach and a quote in addition to your credentials.

Expressions of interest are equivalent to Capability Statements, which at times are called for by various organisations to select consultants for their future projects. Such databases of consultants allow the requesting organisations to put together a short list of consultants and call a closed tender for a particular service or project.

If your Proposal submission is successful you will usually be invited to attend an interview, and if you are selected to provide the required service you may be required to sign a contract for the provision of those services. Whereas it may seem to be a rather bureaucratic process designed for the large organisation, it has some advantages for the service provider. It enables a clear definition of the expectations and methods of payment for services provided. You will need to make sure that the contract does not place unreasonable demands on your practice and that you comply with all its clauses. It is always prudent to read such contracts carefully and to ask a solicitor for a professional opinion so that you clearly understand your contractual obligations.

6.3.2 Where to find tenders

The most common place to find requests for tender is in the major metropolitan and national newspapers. Most editions and especially the weekend papers contain large numbers of such notices. You need to be aware that sometimes calls for Expressions of Interest are published in the main part of the paper rather than in the 'Tender' section. The process of finding the sort of advertisement that is suitable to your practice is rather time consuming. There are many pages of such notices that you need to scan and sometimes you may not find anything of interest for many weeks.

Another more costly but far more efficient way of locating relevant advertisements is to subscribe to a tender search service. You will be informed of the sorts of tenders that you specify are of interest to you either by fax or by mail. You can locate your local search provider in the *Yellow Pages* under 'Management Information Services'.

More recently tender search services have been introduced on the Internet that are available free to users, and instead the requesting organisations are charged for electronic publishing. Some organisations have opted for this service in preference to printed media. They also demand that the submissions are presented in an electronic format. Examples of such a tender service are Tenders Online, which can be found at the Internet address of *http://www.vicnet.net.au/tenders*, and government tenders at *http://www.gems.gov.au.*

6.3.3 How to maximise the probability of success

The process of applying for project work via a tender can be time consuming and akin to writing a job application. You must keep in mind that you will probably be competing against a large number of other applicants. You cannot expect to win each one of them, but you can do quite a lot to increase your chances of winning. Some of the hints to maximise your probability of success are:

- Always obtain the Consultants' Brief and get in touch with the organisation's representative to check if there is any other relevant information.
- Keep to the brief as much as possible in your submission.
- Provide the most relevant experience to the requested project.
- Quote competitively but within your budget to be sure it is actually worthwhile to do the work for your practice.

Find out all you can about the calling organisation. A tender that shows such insight can give your response that extra edge.

7 Selling your practice

The thought of selling your practice may not be high on your agenda at the time of setting it up. To be sure that your ends will be met by your means, it may well provide a useful base from which to decide the structure, size and mode of operation of your practice. The process of your planning will be enhanced by your envisioning what you want your practice to be.

Some practitioners may be satisfied to operate a practice that will cease at the point of their retirement or a change in their career direction; in other words, a transient practice, with its beginning and end determined by their own desire to provide their services in the open market and then withdraw them. Any practice that is inextricably linked to the practitioner's individual identity cannot be sold.

An alternative view you may form is that you would like your practice to transcend your own identity so that it can outlive your personal presence in the market. This sort of thinking will give rise to a vision that will govern the way you approach the building of your practice.

Quite often practitioners, quite by accident, reach the point of thinking about selling their practice. They have developed their practice slowly over the years and built up a reputation in the marketplace, as well as a corresponding flow of clients, referrals or project work. As they grow tired and wish to take a longer break or retire from the private practice lifestyle, they are faced with few options. They can shut their doors, give it to someone else to manage or sell it.

7.1 Valuing your practice

As soon as the idea of selling one's practice is considered, the immediate question on everyone's mind is 'How much is it worth?'. In order to find out the answer, practitioners usually ask their accountant who has been helpful in filling out their taxation return forms. To their surprise they usually discover that their accountant does not really know the answer either, because the accountant knows little about the details of how a psychology practice really works as a business. There are specialist accountants who tackle such questions with the same professional skill as they would any other business. This is where your practice management, particularly in the financial area, will come under unprecedented scrutiny.

Whoever buys a business is essentially buying the right to its future cash flow. So the accountants will look to the future for your practice's ability to produce profits and cash. The only way they can assess this relatively accurately is by looking at the past, and then asking some probing questions to ascertain whether the past experience can be replicated in the future. The factors that may militate against such replication of the past experience will be identified at this stage.

The most immediate indicators that are used by business valuers are the profits. These are directly related to sales and expenses. The simplest rule of thumb formula to estimate the value of the business is to multiply the expected net profit by five. The concept behind such valuation is that it is reasonable to expect a 20% return on one's investment. Hence the profits accumulated over the 5 years should provide this return.

Net profit is obtained from the past records of about 3 to 5 years. If the sales have been unusually low or high during this period, the variations need to be explained and possibly averaged. If you are currently running a practice it may be worthwhile for you to pause at this stage and consider your profitability, as it is one of the fundamental aspects of the business language that will determine the worth of your practice. Even if your profits are hidden in the form of a salary paid to yourself and other directors, there must be a way of proving that your practice is profitable. Otherwise, it will be of no other monetary worth than a non-profit charitable organisation. Not that there is anything philosophically wrong with such organisations. Quite the opposite — they are the backbone of our community and societal values. You just need to ensure that this is what you wanted your practice to become, rather than discovering it by accident, at the end of your private practice career.

The external factors by which the worth of a practice is adjusted revolve around the probability that the business will continue despite the owner leaving the practice. The following issues may be explored as part of this valuation process:

- Is there an established flow of clients?
- Is there some guarantee for the ongoing flow of work?
- Is the range of clients adequately broad?
- Is there an established range of products?
- Will there be a continued demand for the services?
- Is the service likely to lose its appeal to clients?
- Are the contracts secure or likely to be cancelled?

- Are there any more competitors?
- Are the premises securely leased?
- To what extent is the practice dependent upon your personal qualities, reputation and contacts?

If you can demonstrate that the risk of the loss of clients or contracts will be minimal when you depart from the scene, the value of your practice will increase.

7.2 Maximising the value of your practice

Because psychology practices usually do not have stock, plant or equipment, their value is almost predominantly in their goodwill. Goodwill is not a tangible asset; it can vary widely depending on the factors explored above. A common misconception is that a business can always be sold some time in the future. This may not necessarily be so and the worth of your practice will depend to a great extent on the level of your personal involvement in it.

The more the practice is linked to your personal exertion, the less it is worth because the risk of losing clients is greater. Therefore, the best way to maximise the value of its goodwill is to minimise its dependence on your personal input. One way to do this is to ensure that, if you are dealing with large organisations, there are written and signed contracts in place. Such contracts should not be dependent on your presence in the business. You can also begin to deliberately involve other psychologists in your practice so that the referrers of clients will learn not to depend on you personally being involved in the delivery of professional services. At the same time your role should change to ensure that the quality of service does not in any way decrease with your reduced personal involvement.

Your practice worth will therefore depend almost entirely on your business management style. As you invest more time in setting up systems (see Section 5.1) the easier it will be for the practice to function effectively and profitably without you.

7.3 Selling it

The actual process of selling a practice is something one does probably only once in a lifetime. There are a number of issues that will become obvious as you contemplate this move. One of them will probably deal with the issue of privacy and confidentiality.

How does one advertise that the practice is for sale without actually diminishing its value by this very advertising? It is important to locate the buyer without alerting the referrers of your clients so that they would not feel anxious about the stability of your practice. Likewise, it is best not to alert your competitors to the fact that your practice is for sale, to minimise the impact on your market share. At the same time, it is one of the potential competitors who will be the most likely candidate as a buyer. Alternatively, a newcomer into the market may choose to purchase an existing practice instead of starting a new one. One way or another you need to locate the potential buyer.

You can do this by placing an advertisement in the relevant professional newsletters, bulletins or newspapers. As you do so, it is best to keep the details of the practice confidential and describe it in general terms. Such description should be adequate to attract an interested party, and include estimated financial turnover, geographical area and the professional area of endeavour. It is also worthwhile to request assistance from a business trading agent so that the initial filtering of interested parties can take place without disclosing your identity.

7.4 Seeking professional advice

There are business advisers specialising in valuing and selling professional practices, and the first stop for assistance will be your accountant. Your accountant will need to liaise with your agent closely to enable the agent to arrive at the most accurate valuation.

It will be most worthwhile to seek such professional assistance well before considering the sale of your practice, so that you may have enough time to establish its real worth and maximise the sale potential. A government small business advice centre (see Appendix B) and any other qualified business adviser can provide valuable assistance in this area.

By the stage of selling your practice you will have learned that it is important to know your knowledge and skill limitations and close the gap by learning from others. As a practitioner and business owner you will have succeeded to manage your resources so well that they continue to thrive after you have departed.

APPENDIXES

Appendix A Associations

Australian Psychological Society (APS)
PO Box 126
Carlton South, Vic. 3053
Phone: (03) 9663 6166
Fax: (03) 9663 6177

Division of Independently Practising Psychologists (DIPP)
DIPP National Membership Secretary
Australian Psychological Society
PO Box 126
Carlton South, Vic. 3053
Phone: (03) 9663 6166
Fax: (03) 9663 6177

Federation of Privately Practising Psychologists of Australia (FOPPPA)
Vice-President: Mr Radek Stratil
PO Box 191
Goodwood, SA 5034
Phone: (08) 233 6433 or
Pager No. (08) 336 587

Constituent organisations of the Federation:

Australian Capital Territory
The Australian College of Clinical Psychologists — ACT Branch
President: Mr Brian Hodge
PO Box 3070
Weston Creek, ACT 2611
Phone: 0414 285 688

National President: Mr Tom Sutton
Canberra Specialist Centre
161 Strickland Crescent
Deakin, ACT 2600
Phone: (06) 285 2499

New South Wales
The Institute of Private Clinical Psychologists of Australia (NSW)
President: Mr Norman Rees
McCallum Consultants
Level 2, 30 Atchison Street
St Leonards, NSW 2065
Phone: (02) 9439 2255

The Australian College of Private Consulting Psychologists (NSW)
President: Dr John Shea
C/- Psychology Department
University of Newcastle
Callaghan, NSW 2308
Phone: (049) 215 956

Northern Territory
The Association of Private Practising Psychologists
President: Ms Dianne Knox
GPO Box 3002
Darwin, NT 0801
Phone: (089) 881 437

Queensland
The Association of Private Practising Psychologists Queensland
PO Box 290
Toowong, Qld 4066
President: Mrs Susanne Wilkie
Suite 32, 101 Wickham Terrace
Brisbane, Qld 4000
Phone: (07) 3832 5454 or
(07) 3839 9711

South Australia
The Institute of Private Practising Psychologists
President: Ms Denise Keenan
Suite 4, Level 1, 155 King William Road
Hyde Park, SA 5061
Phone: (08) 373 2688

Tasmania
The College of Private Consulting Psychologists (Tas)
President: Ms Desiree Taylor
30A Cascade Road
South Hobart, Tas. 7004
Phone: (002) 241 312

Victoria
Australian College of Private Consulting Psychologists Inc. (ACPCP)
President: Mr Don Burnard
21 Bell Street
Coburg, Vic. 3058
Phone: (03) 9354 0799

Western Australia
The Institute of Private Clinical Psychologists of Australia (WA)
President: Mr Nigel Jones
Suite 9, 209 Warwick Road
Duncraig, WA 6023
Phone: (09) 448 5999

Australian Psychological Association (APA)
GPO Box 2826
Canberra City, ACT 2601
Phone: (06) 281 104

American Psychological Association (APA)
750 First Street, NE
Washington, DC 20002-4242
USA
Phone: (202) 336 5500

British Psychological Association (BPA)
48 Princess Road East
Leicester LE1 7DR
UK
Phone: 0011 44 116 254 9568

Australian Human Resources Institute (AHRI)
2nd Floor, 153 Park Street
South Melbourne, Vic. 3205
Phone: (03) 9699 3733

Australian Institute of Training and Development (AITD)
1/2 Thomas Street
Chatswood, NSW 2067
Phone: 1800 025 239

Australian Society of Clinical Hypnotherapists
PO Box 471
Eastwood, NSW 2122
Phone: (02) 9874 2776

National Speakers Association of Australia
10 Johnson Street
Oakleigh, Vic. 3166
Phone: (03) 9563 4174

Safety Institute of Australia
51–55 City Road
Southbank, Vic. 3006
Phone: 1800 808 380

Appendix B Resource addresses

Commonwealth Government Bookshops

Adelaide
60 Waymouth Street
Adelaide, SA 5000
Phone: (08) 231 0144

Brisbane
Shop 10, City Plaza
Cnr Adelaide & George Streets,
Brisbane, Qld 4000
Phone: (07) 229 6822

Canberra
10 Mort Street
Canberra City, ACT 2601
Phone: (06) 247 7211

Hobart
31 Criterion Street
Hobart, Tas. 7000
Phone: (002) 341 403

Melbourne
190 Queen Street
Melbourne, Vic. 3000
Phone: (03) 9670 4224

Parramatta
Shop 24, Horwood Place
Parramatta, NSW 2150
Phone: (02) 9893 8466

Perth
1st Floor, Albert Facey House
Forest Walk, 469 Wellington Street,
Perth, WA 6000
Phone: (09) 322 4737

Sydney
32 York Street
Sydney, NSW 2000
Phone: (02) 9299 6737

Townsville
277 Flinders Mall
Townsville, Qld 4810
Phone: (077) 215 212

Small business agencies

Australian Capital Territory
Business Services Centre
PO Box 254
Civic Square, ACT 2608
Phone: (06) 205 0770

New South Wales
Office of Small Business
Department of Business and Regional Development
PO Box 242
Parramatta, NSW 2124
Phone: (02) 9895 0555

Northern Territory
Territory Business Centre
Development House
PO Box 4160
Darwin, NT 0801
Phone: (089) 897 916

Queensland
Queensland Small Business Corporation
GPO Box 329
Brisbane, Qld 4001
Phone: (07) 3834 6789

Tasmania
Small Business Services
Tasmania Development and Resources
GPO Box 646
Hobart, Tas. 7000
Phone: (002) 206 752

South Australia
The Business Centre
GPO Box 1565
Adelaide, SA 5001
Phone: (08) 233 4600

Victoria
Small Business Victoria
14th Floor, 55 Collins Street
Melbourne, Vic. 3000
Phone: (03) 9651 9888

Small Business Development Corporation
1st Floor, 100 Exhibition Street
Melbourne, Vic. 3000
Phone: (03) 9655 3350

First Place Business Directions
Ground Floor South
215 Spring Street
Melbourne, Vic. 3000
Phone: (03) 9639 4299

Western Australia
Small Business Development Corporation
GPO Box C111
Perth, WA 6001
Phone: (09) 220 0222

State Psychologists Registration Boards

Psychologists Registration Board of Victoria
PO Box 358, Market Street,
Melbourne, Vic. 8007
Phone: (03) 9629 8722

Psychologists Registration Board of New South Wales
PO Box K599
Haymarket, NSW 2000
Phone: (02) 9281 0834

Psychologists Registration Board of Queensland
GPO Box 2438
Brisbane, Qld 4001
Phone: (07) 3225 2529 or (07) 3225 2505

South Australian Psychological Board
16 Norma Street
Mile End, SA 5031
Phone: (08) 439 669

Psychologists Board of Western Australia
PO Box 263
West Perth, WA 6872
Phone: (09) 321 8499

Psychologists Registration Board of Tasmania
GPO Box 125B
Hobart, Tas. 7001
Phone: (002) 336 773

Psychologists Registration Board of Northern Territory
GPO Box 4221
Darwin, NT 0801
Phone: (089) 992 865

Business Registration Offices

Victoria
Office of Fair Trading & Business Affairs
2nd Floor, 452 Flinders Street
Melbourne, Vic. 3000
Phone: (03) 9627 6200

New South Wales
Department of Consumer Affairs — Business Registration Centre
PO Box 972
Parramatta, NSW 2124
Phone: (02) 9895 0111

Queensland
Office of Consumer Affairs
PO Box 3111
Brisbane, Qld 4001
Phone: (07) 3246 1581

Western Australia
Ministry of Fair Trading — Business Names Branch
GPO Box W2072
Perth, WA 6001
Phone: (09) 321 4344

Northern Territory
Office of Business Affairs
GPO Box 3200
Darwin, NT 0801
Phone: (089) 994 136

Australian Capital Territory
Registrar General's Office — Business Names & Associations
GPO Box 788
Canberra, ACT 2601
Phone: (06) 207 0472

Tasmania
Corporate Affairs Office
GPO Box 249C
Hobart, Tas. 7001
Phone: (002) 332 226

South Australia
State Business and Corporate Affairs Office
GPO Box 1407
Adelaide SA 5001
Phone: (08) 226 0700

Department of Industrial Relations

The federal Department of Industrial Relations has regional offices in each capital city and district offices in the larger states. The addresses of its offices are as follows:

New South Wales
Level 9, North Wing
Sydney Central Building
477 Pitt Street
Sydney, NSW 2000
Phone: (02) 9282 0800

District offices also in:
Coffs Harbour: Phone: (066) 52 1922
Newcastle: Phone: (049) 26 1411
Tamworth: Phone: (067) 66 3028

Victoria
14th Floor
North Tower Rialto Building
525 Collins Street
Melbourne, Vic. 3000
Phone: (03) 9207 8010

District Offices also in:
Bendigo: Phone: (054) 43 8055
Dandenong: Phone: (03) 9794 1050
Geelong: Phone: (052) 21 1699

Queensland
11th Floor
127 Creek Street
Brisbane, Qld 4000
Phone: (07) 3231 2533

District Offices also in:
Townsville: Phone: (077) 72 3299

Western Australia
5th Floor
190 St Georges Terrace
Perth, WA 6000
Phone: (09) 426 4333 (main switch)
Phone: (09) 321 7060 (award inquiries)

South Australia
8th Floor West
Commonwealth Centre
55 Currie Street
Adelaide, SA 5000
Phone: (08) 237 6966

Tasmania
Level 6
83–85 Macquarie Street
Hobart, Tas. 7000
Phone: (002) 31 5912

Australian Capital Territory
MLC Building
8–10 Hobart Place
Canberra City, ACT 2600
Phone: (06) 247 0144

State/territory departments responsible for industrial relations

Each state and territory government is responsible for industrial relations within its own border and each has a department with responsibility for industrial relations issues. The names of each state/territory department and the addresses of its head office are as follows:

New South Wales
Department of Industrial Relations
State Bank Building
1 Oxford Street
Darlinghurst, NSW 2010
Phone: (02) 9266 8888

Victoria
Department of Business and Employment
Nauru House
80 Collins Street
Melbourne, Vic. 3000
Wageline: Phone: (03) 9655 1333

Queensland
Department of Employment, Vocational Education, Training and Industrial Relations (DEVETIR)
Citibank Building
199 Charlotte Street
Brisbane, Qld 4000
Phone: (07) 3323 3733

South Australia
Department of Industrial Affairs
5th Floor
45 Pirie Street
Adelaide, SA 5001
Phone: (08) 207 1999

Tasmania
Department of Industrial Relations Vocational Education and Training
4th Floor, TGIO Building
144 Macquarie Street
Hobart, Tas. 7000
Information and inspection services: Phone: (002) 337 657

Western Australia
Department of Productivity and Labour Relations
2 Havelock Street
West Perth, WA 6005
Wageline: Phone: (09) 481 0647

Northern Territory
Office of the Commissioner for Public Employment
Harbour View Plaza
Darwin, NT 0800
Phone: (089) 99 5511

Australian Capital Territory
Department of Business, the Arts, Sport and Tourism
Employment and Industrial Relations Branch
1st Floor North Building, London Circuit
Canberra City, ACT 2601
Private sector industrial relations: Phone: (06) 205 0306

Appendix C Interesting Internet addresses

Listed below are a sample of Internet addresses that you may find useful. We have not provided a comprehensive list of sites as most of these sites contain many links to other sites. Please note that due to the fluid nature of the Internet, the contents and addresses of sites often change and new sites are continually being created.

Psychology-related sites

Name of site	Internet address
Australian Psychological Society	http://www.bhs.mq.edu.au/aps/
American Psychological Association	http://www.apa.org/
Psychology cyber-synapse	http://rdz.stjohns.edu/~warren/psych
Resources for Psychology & Cognitive Sciences on Internet	http://sasuke.shinshu-u.ac.jp/psych/index-page
Psyched about cyber-space	http://wabakimi.carleton.ca/~dplume/
Psych-guide: A guide to sites relevant to psychology	http://www.designers-int.com/Psychguide
Yahoo Search Engine: Science: Psychology	http://www.yahoo.com/Science/Psychology

Research-related sites

The following addresses are for the World Wide Web only. Telnet may also be used to gain direct access to university library computer catalogues to search for journal articles and books. You may phone specific libraries and ask for their Telnet addresses and login passwords.

Name of site	Internet address
Links to Australian Libraries	http://info.anu.edu.au/ozlib/ozlib
The Electric Library	http://www.elibrary.com/id/19/104/
Mental Health Research Institute	http://daicos.mhri.edu.au/
List of Electronic Journals	http://www.edoc.com/ejournal/
Journal: Current Research in Social Psychology	http://www.uiowa.edu/~grpproc/crisp/crisp
Qualitative research & analysis servers	http://qsr.latrobe.edu.au/Public/WWW/resources

Discussion groups

The following are addresses of World Wide Web sites that contain lists of discussion groups. Discussion groups themselves are accessed using e-mail. For a comprehensive list of discussion groups on psychology-related topics, see Patrick (1995).

Name of site	Internet address
List of Discussion Groups	http://www.nova.edu/Inter-Links/listserv
Search list of Discussion groups	http://www.nova.edu/Inter-Links/cgi-bin/lists
Psychology e-mail lists	http://www.cc.utexas.edu/psycgrad/psycmail

Appendix D A sample business plan structure

Business plan

EXECUTIVE SUMMARY

- Historical background
- Vision and mission statements
- Target market and product/service description
- Key objectives and respective strategies
- Key financial indicators and future estimates

Situational analysis

Historical background
- When and how did the business begin?

Products/Services
- What are you selling?
- Why is there a need for these products/services?
- What distinguishes your products from others?

Target market
- Who are your clients?
- What type of client are they?
- What area are they located in?

Total market
- What is the total estimated market for your products/services in a defined geographical area (e.g. in dollar terms)?
- Is the market you are attracting new or existing?

Other providers
- Who else provides similar products/services to yours?
- How many other relevant providers are there in your area?
- What estimated proportion of the total market and your target market do they service?
- How do their services/products compare with yours — in likeness and quality?

Structure
- How is your business organised?
- Are there other people involved?
- If so, what are their roles in business operations?

Resources
- How do you resource all the functions required by business operations?
- Do you employ other staff/subcontractors?

- Who supplies you with the resources you need?
- Where does your business operate from?

Technology
- What office systems do you have in place?
- What specific technology do you employ for providing your services (computers, psychological tests, software)?
- What equipment do you have in your office/clinic?

Strategic audit

SWOT analysis
- Strengths
- Weaknesses
- Opportunities
- Threats

Current service performance
- How well are your services/products currently provided to your clients, in terms of their quality, market acceptance, flexibility and cost?

Current marketing peformance
- How successful have you been in promoting your services/products in terms of the number of clients, growth, relationships with referrers of clients, and contracts?
- What is the historical background of your marketing performance?

Current financial performance
- How well has the business performed in terms of key financial indicators including income, operating costs, net profit, net assets, and current and long-term liabilities?

Purpose

- Business vision
- Business mission statement
- Basis for growth

Objectives and strategies

Marketing strategy
- Raising public awareness
- Specific marketing campaigns

Service strategy
- Future services and products

Resource strategy
- Human resources
- Technological resources

Financial strategy

- Source of finance
- Cash flow projection

Implementation plan

- Marketing action plan
- Service action plan
- Resource action plan
- Financial action plan

Monitoring and evaluation

Appendix E APS recommended schedule of fees

(Reproduced with permission from the Bulletin of the APS, Volume 18, Issue 1, February 1996, pp 16–17).

APS FEES SCHEDULE
1996 National Schedule of Fees and Item Numbers for Psychological Services

(Based on APS recommended Fee Schedule set in October 1995)

SERVICE DESCRIPTION	SERVICE TIME (Minutes)							
	1-15	16-30[1]	31-45	46-60	61-75	76-90	91-120[2]	
Initial Consultation	—	IO 1 $78	IO 2 $110	IO 3 $142	IO 4 $173	IO 5 $204	IO 6 $269	ITEM NO. RECOMMENDED FEE
Subsequent Consultation	SOB[3] $37	SO 1 $78	SO 2 $110	SO 3 $142	SO 4 $173	SO 5 $204	SO 6 $269	ITEM NO. RECOMMENDED FEE
Psychological Assessment[4]	—	PA 1 $78	PA 2 $110	PA 3 $142	PA 4 $173	PA 5 $204	PA 6 $269	ITEM NO. RECOMMENDED FEE
Clinical Psychological Assessment[5]	—	CA 1 $78	CA 2 $110	CA 3 $142	CA 4 $173	CA 5 $204	CA 6 $269	ITEM NO. RECOMMENDED FEE
Neuropsychological Assessment[6]	—	NA 1 $78	NA 2 $110	NA 3 $142	NA 4 $173	NA 5 $204	NA 6 $269	ITEM NO. RECOMMENDED FEE
Report Preparation[7]	—	RO 1 $78	RO 2 $110	RO 3 $142	RO 4 $173	RO5 $204	RO 6 $269	ITEM NO. RECOMMENDED FEE
Case Conference	—	CO 1 $78	CO 2 $110	CO 3 $142	CO 4 $173	CO 5 $204	CO 6 $269	ITEM NO. RECOMMENDED FEE
Telephone Consultation	—	PO 1 $78	PO 2 $110	PO 3 $142	PO 4 $173	PO 5 $204	PO 6 $269	ITEM NO. RECOMMENDED FEE
Travel Time	—	TO 1 $47	TO 2 $70	TO 3 $94	TO 4 $117	TO 5 $140	TO 6 $165	ITEM NO. RECOMMENDED FEE
Group Consultation (2–9 Clients)	—	GO 1 $17	GO 2 $24	GO 3 $31	GO 4 $42	GO 5 $52	GO 6 $63	ITEM NO. RECOMMENDED FEE *(Per Person)*
Family Group (of 2 Clients)	—	F 21 $40	F 22 $55	F 23 $71	F 2 4 $87	F 25 $102	F 26 $134	ITEM NO. RECOMMENDED FEE *(Per Person)*
Family Group (of 3 or more Clients)	—	F 31 $26	F 32 $37	F 33 $48	F 34 $58	F 35 $69	F 36 $90	ITEM NO. RECOMMENDED FEE *(Per Person)*
Attendance[8] at Court or Legal Briefings[12]	—	LO 1[9] $142	LO 2 $142	LO 3[10] $213	LO 4 $249	LO 5 $9	LO 6[11] $387	ITEM NO. RECOMMENDED FEE

Notes and Guidelines on the Application of the APS National Schedule of Fees & Item Numbers for Psychological Services

The schedule is based on the APS recommended fee of $142 per client contact hour, as determined in October 1995. Note that the schedule is not prescriptive, thus leaving room for negotiations between the psychologist and the individual client. However, it is the fee structure to be used by all APS groups in negotiation with outside bodies for 1996, exempting only special considerations in particular jurisdictions which may necessitate changes to address more specific issues.

Please ensure that your clients are aware of the APS recommended fee for the services provided and your specific charge for the service provided, if this varies from the recommended fee.

Accounts *(for reimbursement from health funds)*

Guideline for preparation of accounts.

The account should show:

- Your **Provider Number** (if relevant, as issued by the relevant fund)
- These words: **Consultation:**
Date:
Item Number:
Name(s) of Person(s) seen:

In order to avoid confusion, you are advised not to show any further detailed description of the service provided as the Item number indicates this.*

- **Australian Psychological Society Recommended Fee** (according to Item number): $
- **Agreed Payable Fee** (as negotiated with the client(s) and if different from the recommended fee): $

* Some health funds are requesting inclusion of diagnostic information on accounts. You should only include this information where there has been an explicit arrangement between the health fund and clients. If this is part of their contractual arrangement, you may be obliged to include such details. Otherwise, it may contravene confidentiality requirements.

Cancellation Fees

Fees for cancellation of appointments made for psychological services can be justified if no replacement service is billed for the lost time. Your policy for the charging of cancellation fees should be discussed with the patient/client or the service requester. Written information detailing your policy on cancellations should be available for clients/referring agencies, e.g., printed information sheet or detailed on appointment cards.

The following is a general guideline only. In the instance of a 46–60 minute service:

0–24 hours notice	*Full fee*
24–48 hours notice	50% of fee
48 hours–7 days notice	25% of fee

Prepared by the APS Directorate of Professional Affairs Advisory Group on Health Rebates. Review of the schedule is due to occur in November 1996. Note that from next year, the schedule and determination of the recommended fee will be aligned with the calendar year. The Advisory Group welcomes feedback on the National Schedule. Submissions and comments may be forwarded to the APS National Office.

PETER COTTON PhD MAPS
Director of Professional Affairs

Footnotes to Fee Schedule Table

1 These fees are calculated on the assumption of 66% productivity i.e. one hour of billable time will involve an additional average of half an hour of associated non-billable professional time (e.g., referral source letters, phone calls, test scoring etc.). This productivity ratio is assumed to decrease slightly for items of less than 46 minutes and increase slightly for items over 60 minutes.

2 The fee rate for services estimated to be of more than 2 hours in duration should be negotiated with the client or referral source. The basis for negotiation should be the APS recommended hourly fee rate.

3 This item is only used for brief client contact related to ongoing management/treatment (e.g., brief client consultation, ward round etc.). NB this item is not to be used for writing letters to referral sources etc.

4 Time spent on face-to-face client interview or testing of intellectual, personality, interests or other capacities or traits for the purpose of educational, vocational or other assessment or guidance.

5 Time spent on face-to-face interview or testing by an appropriately qualified psychologist for purpose of assessment or diagnosis of psychopathology. Note that it is the ethical responsibility of the psychologist to only provide services that are within the limits of the psychologist's area of training and competence.

6 Time spent on face-to-face interview or testing by an appropriately qualified psychologist for purpose of assessment of brain functioning. Note that it is the ethical responsibility of the psychologist to only provide services that are within the limits of the psychologist's area of training and competence.

7 A report is a psychological service that is directly requested by the referring agency or client. Thus, reports prepared for clients are usually done so on the basis of explicit written consent from the client or legal guardian. A report is a structured presentation typically including such components as relevant psychosocial history, history of presenting issues, present condition, test results, opinion and intervention recommendations. Professional letters to medical or other referral agencies concerning treatment needs of the client are not considered to constitute reports (refer to footnote 1).

For clients requesting reports, it is the responsibility of the psychologist to clarify the procedures and costs involved prior to report preparation. For extended reports, it is the responsibility of the psychologist to negotiate fee arrangements with the referring agency prior to preparation of the report.

NB Report preparation time is inclusive of relevant file and document review.

General guideline for report length and item numbers:

RO1	=	1 page*	brief supplementary reports e.g., request for elaboration on a previously submitted report
RO3	=	2–3 pages*	short report
RO5	=	4–6 pages*	standard report
RO6+	=	6+ pages*	extended

** A4 single-spaced typed*

(This guideline is not to be interpreted rigidly and report length and charging arrangements may vary according to the specific requirements of the requesting agency.)

8 Attendance includes waiting time and provision of testimony.

9 Attendance at Court for any time less than one hour is charged at the one hour rate of $142.

10 Times for these services are based on 1.5 × APS recommended fee, to take into account the additional complexity, intensity and disruption of this service.

11 For prolonged attendance items of more than two hours, each additional and consecutive hour after the initial two hours is charged at the rate of $213 per hour (1.5 × APS recommended fee) or by negotiation.

12 Travel time to/from Court or briefings as per Travel items TO1–TO6. Travel times of more than two hours are by arrangement. Motor vehicle travel in excess of two hours to incur the additional cost of 55 cents/per km travelled. Air travel to be business class fare and insurance; accommodation at minimum of 4 star hotel and breakfast.

Appendix F Health rebate schedules: A sample

Fund[1]	Membership category required	Provider number	GP ref. required	Individual rebate	Group rebate	Family rate	Limit per individual	Limit per family
HBA	'Premier' 'E'	Yes Yes	No No	$39 per visit $27 per visit	$13 $9	Nil Nil	$450 pa $400 pa	Nil Nil
MBF	'Extras' 'Health & Wellbeing Services'	Yes Yes	Yes Yes	$24 per visit 80% or 60% of cost	$10 80% or 60% of cost	Nil Nil	$200 pa $375 pa	Nil Nil
Medibank Private[2]	'Super-extras'	Yes	No	$50 — first 4 sessions, $25 — next 6 sessions	Nil	$60 (2 visits)	Varies	$700

Notes

1 There are many other state-based funds and their rebates vary.

2 Rebates vary from state to state.

References and bibliography

APS (1988). Setting up in private practice. *Newsletter of the Australian Psychological Society Victorian Branch*, June.

______ (1994). *Local Networking and Marketing Kit — for APS Members in Independent Practice in Clinical, Counselling and Educational Psychology* Carlton, Vic.: Australian Psychological Society Limited.

______ (1995). *Effective Media Techniques — A Guide to Dealing with the Media*. (1st edit). Carlton, Vic.: Australian Psychological Society Limited.

Blanchard, K. & Johnson, S. (1982). *The One Minute Manager*. London: Fontana/Collins.

Block, P. (1981). *Flawless Consulting*. San Diego: Pfeiffer & Company.

Covey, S.R. (1993). *The Seven Habits of Highly Effective People — Restoring the Character Ethic*. Melbourne: The Business Library, Information Australia.

DEET (1995). *Australia's Workforce 2005: Jobs in the Future*. Department of Employment, Education and Training.

DIR (1995). *Managing Employment and Termination Issues — Practical Help for Employers*. Canberra: Department of Industrial Relations.

Francis, R.D. (1994). *Business Ethics in Australia: A Practical Guide*. Sydney: Law Book.

Francis, R.D. & Cameron, C. (1997). *The Professional Psychology Handbook*. Melbourne: Macmillan.

Gale, A. (1990). Applying psych to the psych degree: Pass with first class honours, or miserable failure. *The Psychologist*, *3*, 483–488.

Gerber, M. (1995). *The E-myth Revisited — Why Most Small Businesses Don't Work and What to Do about It*. New York: Harper Collins.

Kent, P. (1994). *The Complete Idiot's Guide to the Internet*. (2nd edit). Indianapolis: Alpha Books, Macmillan Publishing.

KPMG Peat Marwick (undated). *Starting up and Running Your Own Business — Commercial Banking*. Sydney: Commonwealth Bank of Australia.

Kruithof, J. (1993). *Quality Thinking — How to Implement a Quality Philosophy, in your Thinking and Through Personal Change*. Melbourne: The Business Library, Information Australia.

______ & Ryall, J. (1994). *The Quality Standards Handbook — How to Understand and Implement Quality Systems and ISO 9000 Standards in a Context of Total Quality and Continuous Improvement*. Melbourne: The Business Library, Information Australia.

MacDonald, A. (1996). Crimes Compensation Tribunal and psychologists. *Newsletter of the Australian Psychological Society Victorian Branch*, April, pp. 25–31.

Nathan, G. (1993). *Managing the Franchisor/Franchisee Relationship*. Parramatta, NSW: Franchisors Association of Australia and New Zealand.

Over, R., Parry, A., Geddes, J. & Levens, M. (1985). Psychologists in private practice in Victoria. *Australian Psychologist, 20(3)*, 239–250.

Owens, A.G. (1968). Salaried psychologists in full time employment undertaking part-time practice for a fee. *Australian Psychologist, 3(2)*, 81–88.

Patrick, J. (1995). Technopsych — is knowledge of the Internet really of any relevance or importance to psychologists? *The Bulletin of the Australian Psychological Society, 17(6)*, 9–11.

Samson, D. (1988). *Preparing a Business Plan*. Canberra: Australian Government Publishing Service.

Small Business Victoria (1993). *The Small Business Handbook — How to Start and Successfully Operate a Small Business*. Melbourne: The Business Library, Information Australia.

Stanley, P. (1993). *How to Read and Understand a Balance Sheet — The Plain English Guide*. Melbourne: The Business Library, Information Australia.

Sternberg, R. (1993). *The Psychologist's Companion*, Cambridge University Press.

White, J.R.E. & Sarfaty, P.M. (1970). A Report of the Division's Working Party on Private Practice in Clinical Psychology. *Australian Psychologist, 5(2)*, 184–190.

Whitta, M. (1969). Part time practice. *Australian Psychologist, 4(1)*, 65–68.

Wicks, M. (annual). Subject index to Commonwealth legislation. Sydney: Law Book.

Index